AF241379

A NEW WORLD IN ESSEX

The Rise and Fall of the Purleigh Brotherhood Colony,
1896–1903

Victor Gray

A New World in Essex:
The Rise and Fall of the Purleigh Brotherhood Colony, 1896-1903
published in the United Kingdom in 2019
under the imprint Campanula Books of Leslie Bell
47 Belle Vue Road, Wivenhoe, Colchester, Essex CO7 9LD

ISBN 978-1-869848-24-8

Copyright © Victor Gray 2019

The right of Victor Gray to be identified as the author of this work
has been asserted by him in accordance with the
Copyright, Designs and Patents Act of 1988.

All rights reserved.

No part of this book shall be reproduced or transmitted in any form or by any
means, electronic or mechanical including photocopying, recording, or by any
information retrieval system without written permission of the publisher.

Front cover:
Artwork: A Frosty March Morning, 1904, Sir George Clausen (1852 – 1944).
Photo: © Tate, London 2019.

FELLOWSHIP IS HEAVEN, AND LACK OF FELLOWSHIP IS HELL;
FELLOWSHIP IS LIFE, AND LACK OF FELLOWSHIP IS DEATH;
AND THE DEEDS THAT YE DO UPON THE EARTH, IT IS FOR
FELLOWSHIP'S SAKE THAT YE DO THEM.

WILLIAM MORRIS: THE DREAM OF JOHN BALL, 1888.

CONTENTS

ILLUSTRATIONS

Preface and Acknowledgements

The Purleigh colony has been written about before. When, in 1961, W.H.G. Armytage came to write *Heavens Below*, his seminal history of Utopian experiments in England, Purleigh featured as one of his major examples. In 1978, Professor Michael Holman of Leeds University explored the colony again, this time from the perspective of a specialist in Leo Tolstoy and the spread of his teachings, in a paper entitled 'The Purleigh Colony: Tolstoyan progress in the late 1890s', published as part of a volume of *New Essays on Tolstoy*, edited by Malcolm Jones. The following year, Dennis Hardy set Purleigh in the context of other anarchist communities in his *Alternative Communities in Nineteenth Century England*.

Together these three accounts have ensured that the Purleigh colony regularly appears and is discussed in books, articles and theses on both Utopianism and Tolstoy. Many of these are listed in the Bibliography at the back of this book. Particularly worthy of attention for any reader wishing to pursue further the story of Tolstoy's influence in Britain and beyond is Charlotte Alston's magnificently comprehensive account, *Tolstoy and his Disciples*.

Nearly sixty years on from Armytage's study and forty from Holman's and Hardy's, in an age when so many more sources have become available and accessible, it seemed to me that it was timely to re-explore, for a general audience, the story of this short-lived but influential experiment, setting it more fully into the context of the times and the beliefs that contributed to it and of the location in which it was established; and examining some of the ways in which it left its mark on the later lives of those who participated and on subsequent experiments in 'better living'.

Above all, I thought it important that people living in and near Purleigh got to know of this short moment in history when some of the most progressive political ideas of the time were explored beside hearths in their parish and when the author of *War and Peace* watched, from nearly 2,000 miles away, the playing out of this little drama on their doorstep.

And, after all, is not idealism, whatever its outcomes, always worth remembering and celebrating?

I am grateful for advice and assistance to Steven Potter, local historian of Purleigh, who generously directed me to a number of relevant sources; and to Chris Thornton, Consultant Editor of the Victoria County History of Essex, the staff of the Essex Record Office, the Gloucestershire Archive, the Merseyside Record Office, Croydon Central Library and Leeds University Library, Special Collections.

The following institutions and individuals have given permission for the reproduction of images in their possession: the Croydon Citadel Corps of the Salvation Army, p.23; Steven Potter, p.43; Royal British Columbia Museum and Archives, pp.62 and 82; Essex Record Office, pp. 72 and 91; Stephanie Philpotts, pp. 142 and 143; and Joy Thacker, pp. 41, 44, 95 and 127. Other images are the property of the author or are deemed to be out of copyright.

John Kenworthy's great-great granddaughter, Stephanie Philpotts, has undertaken very extensive and admirably detailed research into the family and has been unfailingly generous with her knowledge and with illustrations for the text.

My greatest debt is to Leslie Bell who has been a stalwart companion in the development of this book, giving generously of his time to read and make valuable suggestions on my draft text and undertaking its typesetting and production with unfailing patience and tenacity.

The story of the Purleigh colony could be told quite simply as that of a group of people living in the 1890s who, convinced that somehow, somewhere, there must be a better way of life than the one they were living, went off and tried to turn that dream into a reality, only to find that it was nowhere near as easy as they thought. That much is certainly true. However, individual hopes and ideas can rarely be divorced from the shifting flurries of thought and feeling that swirl around our heads at any given moment in history. To understand the Purleigh colonists more fully we need to set their story in the context of its time and place: the final years of Victoria's reign.

The 1890s was a more turbulent decade than many. The profile Britain presented to the world was that of imperial might and majesty, fuelled by an advanced industrial economy concentrated in its expanding cities. But beneath that impressive veneer, there were pockets of increasing discontent focused on the plight of those who were seen as the unwitting consequences – or victims – of that headlong rush to economic dominance. The slum-dwelling urban poor had become increasingly visible, their destitution highlighted by social commentators like Charles Booth in his massive survey, *Life and Labour of the People in London*, which had begun to appear in 1889.[1] At the same time, the countryside, already weakened by a lengthy agricultural depression dating back to the 1870s, had been robbed of its youth by the rush to more profitable employment in the industrial cities. Land prices were depressed and fields lay fallow. At the beginning of the 19th century, 80 per cent of the population had been country dwellers; by 1911, 80 per cent were living in urban communities.[2] For those left behind, the economic miracle seemed far removed.

These issues were not new in the 1890s. They had been gathering momentum for decades. Many had proposed solutions. Some had made practical attempts to mitigate the worst social injustices and inequalities. There had been isolated prophets of change – people like John Ruskin, William Morris and, more recently, Leo Tolstoy – but their influence (and their success) had been limited. As the 1880s dissolved into the 1890s an increasing number of writers gave vent to their anger or set out their solutions, some practical, some conceived as utopian alternatives to the present state of affairs. 1888 brought the American Edward Bellamy's *Looking Backward, 2000-1887*, portraying a future where a heavily centralised but benevolent socialist state had swept away the worst horrors of private capitalism and replaced it with sunny vistas and grand architecture amid which the citizens of the year 2000, nurtured by the state and taking advantage of mechanisation to reduce their hours of work, could enjoy the bountiful fruits of their labour. Two years later, William Morris produced his own diametrically opposite vision of utopia, *News from Nowhere*, in which the Thames Valley and London had been transformed into a world of decentralised and locally governed communities, combining the best of town and country, where each individual had a voice and played a part and where the drudgery and dehumanising effects of mass production had been replaced by a rediscovery of the rewards and satisfaction of craft work.

Both of these idealised societies were set far into the future. Other writers were more clearly focused on the present and its failings. 1890 also saw the publication of a highly practical and influential proposal for the immediate relief of urban poverty and distress, William Booth's *In Darkest England*, a searching analysis by the founder of the Salvation Army of the problems of contemporary urban society, with a practical proposal for their amelioration through the establishment in the countryside of 'farm colonies' where the casualties of industrial city life could be re-educated in agricultural skills and prepared for new lives in colonies abroad. Then in 1893 came *Merrie England,* a withering account of contemporary ills by the socialist editor of the *Clarion* newpaper, Robert Blatchford, a small book which set out the principles and ambitions of socialism to massive effect: two million copies of a shilling edition were sold.

Blatchford's book did much to spread among the working classes the idea that socialism presented a viable alternative to the competitive and exploitative landscape of capitalism. Such ideas had their roots far back in the century. But how to bring about the change was a matter of endless debate. There were those who wished to head in the direction Karl Marx had proposed: the collapse or overthrow of capitalism, to be replaced by the State or the People as operators of the levers of the economy. Others shared this direction but sought a less drastic route to their goal, believing in using existing parliamentary systems to place like-minded thinkers in positions of authority so as to gradually bring about a new, more equitable distribution of wealth. For them these were years of progress: from the formation of the first national grouping of socialists, the Social Democratic Federation, in 1883, it was only ten years until Keir Hardie became chairman of a new Independent Labour Party, representing them in Parliament as the first openly socialist M.P. The intervening years had seen dispute and schism, but the achievement was still real and significant. Meanwhile, there were others who rejected the idea of the State altogether and wished to see a 'bottom-up' change to society with small collectives coming together to find alternatives and, ultimately, replacements for capitalist systems. Beneath the broad banner of socialism, then, were gathered a very mixed bag of people and ideas. Communitarians, communists, co-operativists, Christian socialists, Fabians, anarchists were all clustered here, each with a very different vision of the route to betterment. Disagreement was much easier to achieve than harmony.

Socialism, in all its many guises, was by no means the only path trodden by those seeking a better way of life for themselves and for society as a whole. There were those whose route was chosen first and foremost with a view to personal self-improvement, whether or not this arose from established religious beliefs. Some of these sought to work out their salvation by isolating themselves from the world. Others chose the way of selfless service to less fortunate groups in society. By the 1890s that good old Victorian virtue of self-improvement, so widely promulgated by Samuel Smiles in his 1859 best-seller *Self-Help* (by 1904 it had sold a quarter of a million copies), was finding itself entwined – at least in some circles – with the newer notion of 'Progressivism', a liaison which spawned a surprisingly diverse offspring, among them vegetarianism, rational dress (sandals, bloomers, Jaeger woollens, etc.), the Arts and Crafts movement and, above all, a hankering after the countryside as opposed to the satanic mills of British cities, stained by pollution both physical and moral.[3]

There was nothing new about the idea of the redemptive power of nature and the hope that, by resettling people on the land, they would discover a fresh, untainted opportunity to live better, whatever that might mean. The pastoral tradition and the monastic retreat had both been around for centuries, if not millennia. But as the 19th century progressed and the flood of population to the cities, with all its attendant problems, came more often to be seen as detrimental, attention turned increasingly to the countryside as the possible setting for solutions of one kind or another. Not only did it seem untainted by pollution, overcrowding and the social problems that came with them. It also – particularly in its current depressed state – presented something of a blank canvas on which to sketch new visions and play out new experiments. Booth's *In Darkest England* was just one manifestation of this, but one that yielded immediate results. Within months of its publication, the Salvation Army had bought 800 acres in Hadleigh in Essex, overlooking the Thames, as the base for its rural training colony. It was not alone; in 1887, a Mansion House Inquiry into the Condition of the Unemployed had set up a sub-committee to look into the idea of agricultural colonies and there followed a rash of enthusiastic explorations and proposals by bodies like the English Land Colonisation Society and the Home Colonisation Society.

That mix of nostalgia and idealism, frequently spoken of in poetic, political or spiritual terms, occasionally found the soil in which to take root and, for better or worse, became a reality, if only for a brief moment. So, across the century, communities, settlements or colonies had appeared like mushrooms and then vanished. Some had their roots in religious sects or movements, usually led by a messianic figure who saw, in isolation, a route to a New Jerusalem or to a Second Coming. Others were led by men (and they were almost invariably men) with a belief that specific contemporary social evils could be banished given only a clean slate, a plot of land and a group of willing, believing participants. Some set out to achieve egalitarian, self-governing colonies, free of all rule but their own; others saw themselves as paternalistic, securing land and setting the rules by which the hapless and poor could be helped to improve their lot by developing their skills and self-sufficiency.[4]

At the beginning of the century, mill-owner Robert Owen had developed what was essentially a benign working colony at his New Lanark Mills in lowland Scotland, demonstrating that, with humane treatment of a workforce, reinforced by educational and cultural opportunities and charged with a sense of common interest in productivity, wealth could be produced to the benefit of all involved. He and his disciples spent the rest of their lives trying to replicate that experiment in ambitious colonies on both sides of the Atlantic, though nothing matched his early success. In the 1840s, the Chartist Feargus O'Connor believed that by raising the finance to settle large numbers of working class men on their own rural plots they would win the right to the '40 shilling vote' and so gradually sway the course of political history. His Chartist Land Company attracted huge publicity and built five colonies across southern England, only to founder ignominiously in financial collapse.

These were just two of the higher profile experiments, but there were a plethora of smaller scale attempts at colonies across the century. Dennis Hardy, in his *Alternative Communities in Nineteenth Century England,* studied 29 of them in depth and undoubtedly there were many more.[5] Significantly perhaps, a third of those he analysed date from the last decade of the century, reflecting the intensification of 'progressive' thinking described above.

This then is the context in which to view the Purleigh colony, just one in a long line of hopes but very much a product of the historical moment. Like so many others, its life was comparatively short and its traces on the ground today are few, but the ripples that spread out from it ran wide and some lasted long into the next century.

Chapter 1

The Groundwork

The winter of 1896 was probably no longer, no colder, no wetter than any other. It just seemed so to the three men huddled around a small fire in a cottage deep in rural Essex. None of them had been born to this way of life. Now here they were, struggling to keep warm on a cold winter night, exhausted by a long day's digging in the fields.

What kept them going was a sense of mission and a burden of responsibility. These men were pioneers, sent out to prepare the way for a social experiment that might challenge the whole basis on which late Victorian Britain had been built.

If there were occasional moments of doubt or recrimination as the fire burned low and the draughts took hold, if there was blame to be laid at the feet of anyone, that man was John Coleman Kenworthy, the man who had brought them here.

J.C. Kenworthy was a Liverpudlian businessman turned questor-after-truth. Born in Everton in 1861, the son of a ship's captain, he had started his adult life as a commission clerk, gradually building a role for himself in the business world, marrying and starting a family.[1] But there was a part of Kenworthy that became increasingly unhappy with his lot. Like so many others at the time, he seems to have been all the while wrestling with an unsatisfied yearning towards a better life and a better society.

Among the most powerful influences on Kenworthy were the writings of John Ruskin. His withering critique of contemporary society and concern for restoring the dignity of labour had led to the formation of his Guild of St George

John Coleman Kenworthy photographed in 1896

in 1871, set up to acquire land on which communities of workers could rediscover the possibility of living close to nature, with dignity and shared aspirations. Ruskin had set out his vision in typically elegant and beguiling words in his *Fors Clavigera: Letters to the Workmen and Labourers of Great Britain*, published between 1871 and 1884:

We will try to make some small piece of English ground, beautiful, peaceful, and fruitful. We will have no steam-engines upon it, and no railroads; we will have no untended or unthought-of creatures on it; none wretched, but the sick; none idle, but the dead. We will have no liberty upon it; but instant obedience to known law, and appointed persons: no equality upon it; but recognition of every betterness that we can find, and reprobation of every worseness. When we want to go anywhere, we will go there quietly and safely, not at forty miles an hour in the risk of our lives; when we want to carry anything anywhere, we will carry it either on the backs of beasts, or on our own, or in carts, or boats; we will have plenty of flowers and vegetables in our gardens, plenty of corn and grass in our fields, and few bricks. We will have some music and poetry; the children shall learn to dance to it and sing it; perhaps some of the old people, in time, may also.[2]

It was a vision which would settle in Kenworthy's mind as it did in the minds of thousands of others living in the hubbub of late Victorian industrial cities at that time. When a Liverpool Ruskin Society was formed in 1883, he was quick to join. In the event, Ruskin's attempts to turn into reality his vision of a rural community of spirit proved less than successful, but it was no doubt the starting point for Kenworthy's search for a pattern of belief shared with like-minded souls and turned into a practical reality as an idealistic community.[3] It would remain with him as he started a family and pursued his life in commerce.

At the same time another thread of interest was developing in Kenworthy's mind. In about 1882 he joined the socialist movement.[4] "Land Nationalisation and the Abolition of Interest seemed to me then … to furnish a sufficient programme for social reform", he would later write.[5] Thereafter, throughout the 1880s, he sustained an active involvement with progressive groups in and around Liverpool. He was quick to organise a local branch of the Christian Socialist Society when it was founded in 1886 and early in 1890 he was in contact with William Morris, a founder-member of the Socialist League, persuading him to agree (somewhat reluctantly) to give a series of lectures in the city, one on Gothic art and two on socialism. [6]

Nevertheless there was still something missing: "Nothing in modern teachings, nothing in the labours of Socialists and others for social reform, satisfied the demand in me for a sufficient truth, and for a line of activity that should be felt as finally right. At last I found both those desiderata; I found them in the Christian Gospel".[7] The date of this new awakening Kenworthy would later place at about 1886. But his new-found attraction to Christian teaching was actually very deeply rooted in and coloured by both the experience of his business life and the lessons of his socialist reading. He had, he explained, come to see a marked contradiction between, on the one hand, the worthy behaviour of men in their commercial transactions, where they were informal and based upon trust and honesty, and, on the other, the dishonesty displayed when transactions were bound by and conducted on the basis of legal contract. "I understood, literally in one moment, fourteen years ago, the meaning of the saying: 'Forgive us our debts, as we forgive those who are indebted to us'. *That prayer, truly made, is for the abolition of all laws and powers of coercion by which debts are secured and collected".* [8] He became, in short, a believer in resistance to all forms of imposed authority and placed his faith in the moral convictions of the individual heart and mind as urged by Jesus Christ. Kenworthy felt he had discovered an important –

indeed a central - truth, but he searched in vain for others who had seen this light. "I found myself alone, in amazement". He would have to wait a few more years to find a fellow-spirit and, when it came, it would be a meeting of minds which would eventually change the course of his life.

That moment arrived in 1890 when Kenworthy came across and read Leo Tolstoy's *My Religion* and part of his *What To Do?*[9] Born in 1828 into an aristocratic family, Tolstoy had led a decidedly rakish life until, in his thirties, he became increasingly influenced both by Christ's teachings and by anarchist thought. He retired to the family estate at Yasnaya Polyana and dedicated himself to his writings and to the pursuit of his newly adopted beliefs. At their heart was a core of Christianity, but a Christianity stripped of all dogma and ceremony and based on the simple principles of the Sermon on the Mount, with its blessings upon the meek, the merciful, the pure in heart and the peace-makers. From this he evolved his advocacy of adopting simplicity of life, even asceticism, empathy for others, particularly the poor and humble, and pacifism taken to the level of unswerving non-resistance. Seeing all forms of government and religion as based on control and the threat of violence, he espoused a form of anarchism (though he resisted all such labels), turning his back on all forms of authority and placing his central focus on the individual's search for self-perfection from within.

In 1890 Tolstoy's works were just becoming known in translation in Britain. Though *War and Peace* dated back to the 1860s and *Anna Karenina* to 1877, neither was published in English until 1886, at the same time as the first translations of some of his philosophical works were appearing. It was these that struck Kenworthy so forcefully, resonating in the profoundest way in a mind already predisposed to these issues. "I was surprised and glad", he later wrote, "to find a mind working on my own lines, but in advance, with a wider and maturer discussion".[10]

It was not the most timely moment. On Christmas Eve 1890, with his wife and three children (the youngest under a year), he sailed for America where a new post awaited him.[11] The family settled in Englewood, New Jersey, just over the Hudson river from New York.[12] His work would take him westward across America, buying and selling.[13] Not that he left behind his philosophical or political interests. While in New York he quickly gravitated towards like-minded groups, making sufficient ground to be identified, together with a fellow Englishman, William C. Owen, and an anarchist architect, John H. Edelmann, as the founders of the Socialist League, an anarchist group which broke away from the Socialist Labor Party in 1892 and was clearly based on the model of the British Socialist League, established by William Morris eight years before. At one point he asked Morris to visit New York to lecture. This time he was turned down.[14]

All this while, however, the impression that Tolstoy's work made on Kenworthy grew and developed, reinforced by more reading of his works.[15] "I knew myself to be at one with, and indebted to, the man who had understood the Gospels as I also had done", he recalled.[16] Within eighteen months he had decided to leave behind what he referred to as 'the bitter service of commerce' and return to England to take on a new life, dedicated to following at least some of the paths mapped out by Tolstoy.

The family arrived in the Port of London at the end of July 1892.[17] Back in England with a new sense of purpose, Kenworthy headed straight for the notoriously impoverished and overcrowded east end of London. Just as Tolstoy had followed his own teaching by devoting himself to the understanding and care of the peasants on his estate at Yasnaya

Polyana, so Kenworthy seemed bent on alleviating the condition of some of the poorest in England. It was less than ten years since a Congregational minister, Andrew Mearns, had shocked society with his exposé of the depths of poverty in the capital's slums, published in 1883 as *The Bitter Cry of Outcast London*. In its wake, a number of 'mission settlements' had been set up in the most deprived parts of the capital. The first, Toynbee Hall, the initiative of an Anglican curate, Samuel Barnett, had set out to bring young men - possible future leaders of the country - from Oxbridge colleges to London, to live and work alongside the poor, to improve their living conditions, providing them with education and opportunities for cultural, social and sporting activities. Other denominations soon followed, among them the Congregational church which, in 1890, established the Mansfield House University Settlement in the dockland district of Canning Town. It quickly set up a Men's Club offering recreational facilities and went on to develop a range of educational classes and opportunities for mutual self-improvement: among them a penny bank, a loan society and a sick benefit society.[18]

The Mansfield House University Settlement, Canning Town

This was where Kenworthy headed. Why he chose Mansfield House is not clear. He had been raised as a Methodist but by now, under the influence of Tolstoy's renunciation of religious affiliation in favour of an entirely personal engagement with Christian morality, he would probably have denied any denominational allegiance. What is certain is that this first exposure to the deplorable conditions of the East End strengthened his determination to dedicate himself to improving the lot of his fellow beings. By 1893 he was acting as secretary to a special committee set up by a number of interested organisations to report on Farm Labour Colonies and Farm Settlements as a means of removing the poor and unemployed out of the city into rural surroundings where they could learn new skills. The committee's report resulted in the foundation, within months, of the English Land Colonisation Society. Kenworthy became its secretary. By October the Society was seeking private sector partners to offer land and capital for a trial colony for the unemployed, who would be identified and provided by one of the London Boards of Guardians. [19]

Here then was the busily engaged social reformer, committee man, writer, activist. But though he had taken his first steps along a new road, his reflections on Tolstoy's thinking continued to mature. In July 1893, while still in Canning Town, he put the last touches to a book, *The Anatomy of Misery: Plain Lectures on Economics*, setting out his analysis of the wrongs of a capitalist system which continued to deprive working people of their just share of the fruits of the world.[20] At times in this book his keen sense of injustice verges on righteous anger but, whereas others at the time saw the only solution as lying in the complete overthrow of the political and economic system, Kenworthy, in his concluding chapters, rejects violent revolution as having, on historical evidence, always substituted one form of tyranny for another. "Violence begets violence; the successful mob is the tool of the military dictator. Robespierre is the prophet of Napoleon". It could have been Tolstoy speaking.

He proceeded equally to dismiss mainstream political action as the way forward, arguing that this had only managed in the past century to scratch away at a small corner of the injustices of the system. "Those who are most intimate with the Labour movement best know the helplessness of Labour against a corrupt Propertied-Class Parliament; they know that the only successful Political Action is that which will result from the creation of a sound Public Opinion, that shall sweep away the whole present machinery of Government".[21] It is to the gradual creation of that public opinion that he turns in his final few pages. Only through personal amelioration, through a life lived according to the laws of fair and unselfish social behaviour, can the beginnings of a solution be found. "Economic principles are, as we have seen, governed by Moral considerations. Morals are, finally, dependent upon our conception of the solution of the great mystery. What is to become of us hereafter? That is, Morals are based upon Religious Belief. Which is as much as to say, that Economic questions are, finally, Religious questions".[22]

This was at the core of Tolstoyan thinking and it was that thinking that no doubt took Kenworthy next towards the Fellowship of the New Life, a loose (and fairly small) group of like-minded souls established in 1883 with the lofty goal of 'the cultivation of a perfect character' through the subordination of material things to spiritual matters. By the time Kenworthy came to it, it was a body which was decidedly on the wane. A good deal of its initial energy had gone when, a year after its creation, the Fellowship had split, a substantial part of its membership breaking away to form the Fabian Society, dedicated to bringing about a better life through political engagement rather than through simple personal improvement. But the pursuit of spiritual and practical self-improvement, the replacement of the spirit of competition by an unselfish pursuit of the common good, the adoption of a simple life-style and the bringing together in a single life of manual labour and intellectual enquiry: these were all now quite definitely Kenworthy's interests and goals. In July 1894 he was invited to join the Fellowship's committee and throughout 1894 and 1895 became a regular contributor to its journal, *Seed-Time*. The beliefs he promulgated there were passionately expressed:

> The part of our 'programme' which differentiates us from others who seek after the ideal society, is the determination that, let the world go in such way as it pleases, we, each one for his own part, for 'the salvation of his own soul' must live honestly and fraternally towards all men. That principle of conduct, seemingly so individualistic, is really the basic principle of the Kingdom of Heaven which Jesus and all prophets have foreseen.[23]

But they were also hammered into a programme of practical action, in which groups of families, or 'neighbourhoods' would act together to create working communities aiming to achieve self-sufficiency. They would together acquire agricultural land for use as 'colonies' to which members could be sent to learn new and productive skills. This was land colonisation as envisaged by the Land Colonisation Society but now charged with the theology of Tolstoy.

1894 was a year in which all Kenworthy's developing thinking and activities seemed to come together in new commitments. The most important of these came through his new-found friendship with an Irish Congregational minister, John Bruce Wallace, who in 1892 had turned an ailing Congregational church in Southgate Road, Hackney, into what he called the Brotherhood Church, committed to a programme based upon Christ's teachings in the Sermon on the Mount, of direct social action to improve the lot of the

The Brotherhood Church, Southgate Road, Hackney

suffering and under-privileged. This was not a poor area; a planned estate from the 1820s and '30s now housed fairly well off middle-class and tradesman families, but Wallace, who would have described himself as a Christian Socialist, may have decided that these were exactly the hearts and minds he needed to change. For four years before coming to London he had been publishing his own magazine, *Brotherhood*, with hard-hitting articles on poor social conditions and descriptions of social experiments around the world.[24] The gathering he organised in December 1892 to publicise the new role of the Southgate Road church attracted such figures as Keir Hardie, the newly elected first Labour M.P., and Ben Tillett, the union leader and hero of the 1889 London Dock Strike.

It is possible that Kenworthy, living as he then was in Plaistow, just a few miles away, and engaged with the Congregational Mansfield House in Canning Town, was there on that day. If not, he may well have attended at least some of the regular 'Social Questions Conferences' which Wallace led in the church on Sundays in the months following. Certain it is that some time shortly after the birth of the Brotherhood Church Wallace and Kenworthy grew to know and respect each other. 'My friend, J.C. Kenworthy, a man of extensive business experience and ardent Christian Socialist' is how Wallace came to describe him when, just over a year later, he took the next step in his programme and, on 19 January 1894, launched the Brotherhood Trust, with the two of them as initial trustees.[25]

Chapter 2

The Brotherhood Ideal

The beginnings of the Brotherhood Trust may have been small but the vision, set out in a sort of manifesto signed by the trustees, was nothing short of grand.[1] The Trust would set up interlinked businesses from which both workers and customers would benefit: the first by earning a wage no less than the trade union rate current at the time for comparable work, the customers by being offered old-age pensions and sickness benefits in proportion to the scale of their purchases. The fund which was to achieve this would be created from the profits of the enterprises overall. Instead of paying dividends like the now well established co-operative societies, profits would be ploughed into the purchase of land on which co-operative farms could be set up to supply goods to the Trust's shops. The hope was that those who associated themselves with the Trust would become, in the course of time, both workers for the Trust and customers for its goods. As the numbers grew, so the linked businesses would expand outwards across the country until they provided a viable co-operative alternative to what Kenworthy called the Mammon System, the profit-driven and exploitative commercial world which created disproportionate wealth in a few hands at the expense of an impoverished under-class. "It is a plan", wrote Wallace, "for swallowing up the profit-mongering industry and commerce of the world, which keep the many mere wage-slaves and drudges, and for transmuting it, by a perfectly constitutional and peaceful revolution, into a fraternal organisation for mutual enrichment and security". His plan of attack envisaged a pyramid-system of recruitment which might achieve a million members in four years.[2]

On the morning after this trust deed was signed, the doors opened on the first of the Brotherhood enterprises. The ripples which were to reach out across the land were to start their journey at No. 1 Downham Road, less than a quarter of a mile from the church, on the corner of Kingsland Road, a bustling thoroughfare leading south into the City. Money had been given interest-free by an unidentified well-wisher to allow this start to be made and a supply of bread and groceries was available for the first customers. Within months it had extended its stock to include 'bread, grocery, provisions, etc., oils, tinware, earthenware, brushes, etc., coals', and arrangements had been made to link with a local tailor and a bootmaker in nearby Kingsland Road.

As has been mentioned, a key part of Wallace and Kenworthy's plans for spreading the Brotherhood structure was the founding of new groups which would, in due course, link together in mutual exchange of both goods and markets to form a 'Co-operative Commonwealth'. Once the co-operative venture from Wallace's Southgate Road church was up and running, it was not long before new Brotherhood Churches followed in Forest Gate, Queen's Park and Walthamstow and later in Streatham, Edgware Road and Kentish Town. But now it was Kenworthy's turn to play a role. He left behind his work in Canning Town and moved his family to Croydon.

South of and less than ten miles from the heart of London, Croydon had experienced the full force of metropolitan growth during the 19th century. From less than nine thousand inhabitants in 1801 it was now, in the 1890s, home to more than a hundred thousand. There had been the inevitable problems of slum housing and inadequate services that came with population growth on such a scale but there were also areas of the borough which were now sought-after leafy middle-class residential areas. As a result, all manner of men could be found here. It had become just the sort of environment – rapidly changing and thus exposed to new problems and new ideas – in which activists and idealists came together to solve (or at least discuss) the world's inadequacies and dilemmas. It was now something of a hub for the activities of the Fellowship of the New Life and so, perhaps, was already known to Kenworthy. There had been a branch of the Social Democratic Federation here since the mid-1880s and nearby Thornton Heath had been one of the first places in the country to open a branch of the Independent Labour Party when it had been formed in 1893. In the same year a Croydon Socialist Society had been established in the West Croydon Temperance Hotel. Already the Fellowship (now known as the New Fellowship) had opened a 'free church' in the town and now the new-born Brotherhood movement found its way here too.

Church Street, Croydon, in the 1890s

On 3 June 1894 a new Croydon Brotherhood Church held its first service. The following Saturday the Croydon

Socialist Society organised a visit and address by Keir Hardie, then the only Independent Labour MP to be sitting in the Commons. The wagonette in which he rode to the public park on Duppas Hill, on the edge of the town, carried a large advertisement for the opening of the new Brotherhood Church; there could have been no better way to ensure that the local press reported its arrival.[3]

Many years later, Nellie Shaw would recall that "A few of us – five men and two women – started a group in Croydon which we designated 'The Croydon Brotherhood Church' – the latter word being used in the sense of a number of people inspired by a common aim but with no religious or theological imputation".[4] Its first Management Committee was drawn from a broadly 'progressive' background. All socialist in inclination, they included Mary Grover, a Theosophist, Fabian and Suffragist; Nellie Shaw, who before coming to the Church had involved herself with the Fabian Society, the Independent Labour Party and the Croydon Socialist Society; and Fred Muggeridge (father of Malcolm Muggeridge), who would go on to be the first Labour member on Croydon Council.[5]

Through Wallace and through the Fellowship of the New Life, this group knew of Kenworthy and his writings on social questions and in May 1894 they appointed him their first 'Honorary Pastor'. With his wife and three children he moved to a small house in the Pitlake Bridge area, one of the poorer parts of Croydon, and took up his new challenge.

Just as Wallace had taken over an earlier church building, so did the Croydon group, securing the use for their meetings of what had been built in 1872 for the Christian Mission (later renamed the Salvation Army) and abandoned by them in 1887 in favour of a new Citadel.[6] It was at No. 46 Tamworth Road, close to the centre of the town and at the heart of the mass of terraced housing which had grown up to meet the needs of the expanding population.

The Salvation Army's Croydon Christian Mission, later the Brotherhood Church

Kenworthy quickly adopted Wallace's practice of Sunday Social Questions Conferences, starting at 3 o'clock and followed by tea and then an 'evening service' at seven with 'hymns or social songs, readings and prayer, a sermon from Kenworthy and discussion'.[7] One acerbic letter in the *Croydon Advertiser* described Kenworthy as 'this red-tied, round-shouldered, weak-chested melancholy-looking young pastor' but, though clearly not in sympathy with his views, the writer was nevertheless impressed by the vehemence of his condemnation of land-owners, capitalists and (quoting Kenworthy's original words) the church: "The Churches and Chapels at present exist for the sole purpose of dodging the property question, and hoodwinking the people, by holding out to them the promise of a mansion in Heaven, for the privilege of robbing them on earth".[8] No-one ever accused Kenworthy of weakness of expression.

Over the next year attendances grew till they were approaching a hundred. [9] The sessions were lively and varied in theme. The first year included addresses on Theosophy, on Thomas Lake Harris, the founder of the Fellowship of the New Life, and on 'The Subjection of Women'. Varied too were the participants. One attender, looking back a decade later, remembered these sessions as 'a Hecklers' Paradise'.[10] Another recalled: "Every kind of 'crank' came and aired his views on the open platform, which was provided every Sunday afternoon. Atheists, Spiritualists, Individualists, Communists, Anarchists, ordinary politicians, Vegetarians, Anti-Vivisectionists and Anti-Vaccinations – in fact every kind of 'anti' had a welcome and a hearing, and had to stand a lively criticism in the discussion which followed".[11]

In many ways Wallace's vision for a Brotherhood Church as the base from which social and practical action would spring was lived out more fully in Croydon than anywhere else. Within a short time the Croydon meetings would spawn a choir, youth meetings, physical exercise classes, a rambling club, a book club and a Social Questions class, which began by reading and discussing Robert Blatchford's socialist polemic *Merrie England*. Classes were also provided for boys and girls, led by a team of keen volunteers. But perhaps more significantly, it moved quickly in the direction of co-operative enterprise, using the model of Wallace's north London foundation. On 10 November, barely six months after the Church came into being, a Croydon Brotherhood Trust Store was opened in the shop which adjoined the Kenworthy's house at 'Hollycombe', No. 2 Pitlake, West Croydon, a half mile or so to the west of the Church. Open from seven to ten in the evenings, it was run by members of the Brotherhood Church under the watchful secretaryship of Arthur St. John, a former Captain in the Inniskilling Fusiliers who, like

Kenworthy, had been converted by reading Tolstoy, this time on the voyage home from Burma. Within weeks it was being proudly boasted that 'Beginning with Tea and Labour Papers and Publications, goods such as Stationery, Tobacco, Sugar, Dried Fruit and Soap have been added week by week'.[12] Down below there was a basement, converted into a reading room, named 'The Rendezvous' and open to all every evening for the study of subjects linked to the Church's message.

The store's suppliers were chosen on ethical grounds to reflect the Brotherhood's goal of a co-operative and interdependent network. Its jam, for example, came from the Methwold Farm Colony in Norfolk, set up in 1889. Cocoa and chocolate were supplied by the London Productive Society, based in Thames Ditton and describing itself as 'the co-operative cocoa and chocolate makers', while needles came from the Alcester Productive Society, set up by the Alcester Co-operative Society in 1888 to manufacture needles (a speciality of the town) on a co-operative basis. Orders could also be taken for items of clothing, produced by a local tailor, Gilbert Tarry, from cloth supplied by the co-operatively owned Scottish Tweed Manufacturing Society in Selkirk. It must have felt as though the makings of the national web of co-operation were already in place. By the autumn of 1897 it was able to offer:

> Groceries, fruit, flour and semolina (which the manufacturers claim to make from pure English wheat). A speciality is made of pulse, grain and other vegetarian foods. Books and stationery; labour, socialist, vegetarian and other advanced periodicals and literature. Goods delivered by cart every Friday. Arrangements have been made with a

local tailor for clothes to be made with co-operatively produced materials. Also for natural undyed wool clothing.[13]

Advertisements for the Croydon Brotherhood Industries, *The New Order*, Sept. 1897

The shop was just the start. The Croydon Brotherhood Dressmakers followed, managed by Church member Nellie Shaw, who had up until then been in business with her widowed mother but, fuelled by a pronounced social conscience, had grown to dislike selling cheap goods 'produced by sweated labour'. The Dressmakers would, when opportunity arose, specialise in the 'rational dress' which was favoured by the free-thinking progressives of the day as a

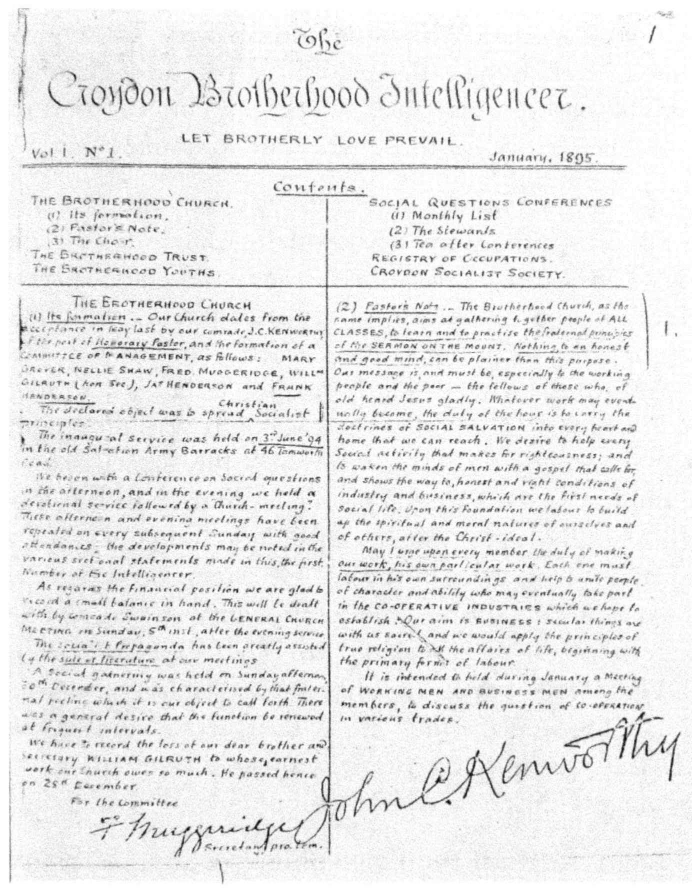

The first edition of
The Croydon Brotherhood Intelligencer, January 1895

visible reaction to the fussiness of late Victorian fashion; 'Dress cut and fitted on scientific principles (artistic and rational costumes specially designed)', read one advertisement issued in September 1897.[14] Then came a laundry, set up in a house in Dryden Road where two members were already making and mending boots and sandals for Brotherhood members, and soliciting custom from members of the church to help them achieve their goal of working fully within the co-operative framework. A Brotherhood Bakery was soon being planned. Even Kenworthy played his part in extending the range of services available, offering 'a limited amount of carpentering work for those who care to employ him'.[15]

Key to the church's ambitions was the work of spreading the word. In January 1895 Kenworthy issued the first edition of *The Croydon Brotherhood Intelligencer*, intended as a monthly review of progress as well as a platform for preaching and discussing the main tenets of Brotherhood. The first edition set the tone unambiguously in its 'leader', described as 'Pastor's Notes'. The aim of the Church was 'the gathering together of people of ALL CLASSES [his capitals], to learn and to practise the fraternal principles of the SERMON ON THE MOUNT. Nothing, to an honest and good mind, can be plainer than this purpose'. He went on immediately, however, to describe the anti-capitalist goal of the Brotherhood Trust, speaking of 'The CO-OPERATIVE INDUSTRIES which we hope to establish. Our aim is BUSINESS: secular things are with us sacred and we would apply the principles of true religion to all the affairs of life, beginning with the primary forms of labour'.

Pretty soon, all the Brotherhood enterprises would be grouped together on the back page of the *Intelligencer* under the headline 'Co-operative Industries'. At the same time a Registry of Occupations was set up with the names of 34 tradesmen and professionals from the building trades, publishing, teaching and office work who had signed up to offer their services to the co-operative goal.[16]

The first edition of the *Intelligencer* was a simple four-page handwritten document, mechanically reproduced in small numbers, but by the second month it was being printed by a sympathetic local printer, Jonathan Row, in Selsdon Road. Soon it was being produced on a press set up in the basement of the Brotherhood Store, marking the birth of the Croydon Brotherhood Publishing Company. From these beginnings and in due time the company would come to boast a London office at 26 Paternoster Square and become the channel for publishing a number of the papers read at the Social Questions Conferences and for Kenworthy's own Tolstoyan publications (of which more later).

The Waddon Hotel, once 'Brotherhood House', seen in 2017

Perhaps most ambitious among the Church's programme of expansion was the acquisition of a large nearby property, built in 1885 as the Waddon Temperance Hotel, leased and reopened in November 1895 as Brotherhood House, 'a centre of practical Socialism and a training house for Socialists'.[17]

Run as a co-operative operation with Walter and Mary Older in day-to-day charge, it was to function as a home for young men disposed to explore co-operative living and working. Board and lodging cost thirteen shillings a week.[18] In due course, many of the other Brotherhood enterprises – the store, the dressmaking business and other new ventures in tailoring and bootmaking – were consolidated in this building.

Meanwhile efforts were being made to involve the church in the life of the wider Croydon community. Classes were held in the evenings, open to all and teaching drawing, clay modelling, handicrafts and military drill. But engagement needed to run deeper than mere educational support. In pursuit of both its Christian and its Socialist goals, the Church quickly established an Unemployed Committee to 'investigate, agitate and help' the dire condition of unemployment in the area. By February 1895 church members had undertaken a census of sample streets in the town which concluded, by extrapolation, that 32 per cent of the working population of the town were unemployed. The following months were spent in disseminating this knowledge by flyer and by letters to the press and relevant authorities.

To make matters worse for the poor the early months of 1895 were bitterly cold. There have only been three colder winters in Britain since that year. By February the Thames had frozen over – the last time this occurred. All over the country transport was disrupted and unemployment soared. In Croydon, the doors of the Brotherhood Church were thrown open and in the region of 5,000 free meals provided for the needy.[19]

This was an impressive set of achievements in what was barely two years from the signing of the Brotherhood Trust manifesto. Indeed, such was the local success of the Church that the *Intelligencer* was able to report in July that new groups were 'in formation' at Penge, Selhurst, Sydenham, Thornton Heath, Wallington, South and West Croydon and South Norwood.[20] At the end of 1895, however, one important goal set out in the manifesto remained to be fulfilled: that of acquiring some productive land from which to supply dairy and farm crops to the Trust customers and workers, thus completing the circle of self-sufficiency. In the light of his earlier work for the Colonisation Society with its 'back to the land' belief in the economic and moral power of a return to the soil to solve many of society's problems, Kenworthy was keen to move forward on this. The dire situation in Croydon had only strengthened his view. In February, in the same week as 500 unemployed men marched through the streets to the Town Hall to petition the Mayor over their distress, Kenworthy, working from the Bible text 'Why stand ye here all the day idle; and they said unto him, Because no man has hired us', drove home his message in his Sunday 'sermon': "though there was plenty of land to cultivate and plenty of tools to work with, yet men could not bring the two together without being hired by some owner of land or capital". Co-operative working of the land to the common good was the answer.

The very next month, the *Intelligencer* published a notice that an action committee had been formed to look into 'acquiring a good-sized piece of land in some pleasant situation near Croydon'. Among its members were Arthur St. John and the two joint managers of the Brotherhood Store, James Henderson and David Frazer. In April, Kenworthy took the opportunity to publicise their ambition in *Seed-Time*, the regular journal of the Fellowship of the New Life:

Some of our members are now seeking for a piece
of land, five acres or thereabouts, in our
neighbourhood, where we can pitch 'Brotherhood
Camp' [and where] we may, during the summer,
inaugurate our longed-for exodus to a life of honest
labour in the country, by days and afternoons of
holiday-making upon our own acres. Next year it is
hoped serious cultivation may begin, for the supply
of produce which our store will sell. In such ways, a
new society, rid of old cruelties and dishonesties,
may be built up; the point of doubt is, Have we
sufficient faith and unselfishness to give ourselves
up to the work?

Over the summer Kenworthy returned, in the columns
of the *Intelligencer*, to the theme of working the soil as the
clearest expression of Tolstoy's 'bread labour' concept,
essentially the principle of each man earning and producing
his daily bread through manual labour. To prepare the way, the
enterprising St. John was sent off to find out exactly what
skills might be needed to run just such a smallholding. He
travelled to the north, to Starnthwaite in Westmorland, where
a Unitarian minister, Herbert Mills, the author of *Poverty and
the State*, had started a 'home colony' of 127 acres in 1892 to
provide productive and satisfying labour for the unemployed
as an alternative to the workhouse. By the time St. John
arrived considerable strides had been made in clearing the
land to make way for fruit trees, but there were also emerging
problems as some of the colonists who had come forward in
the hope of finding themselves part of a colony run on
socialist or at least co-operative lines found that they were
really part of a social experiment in poverty alleviation run by
a dictatorial theorist.[21]

It took longer perhaps than anyone had expected to find a suitable piece of land at a price the Trust could afford. They were up against a problem that frequently besets those in search of self-sufficient and self-financing projects. Financial self-sufficiency may be achievable once you are up and running, but to get to that point you need up-front finance. The Trust Manifesto had foreseen the various enterprises making sufficient profit to allow them to acquire and expand. But at Croydon they were far from being in that position. The Brotherhood Store, for example, successful as it may have proved to be in its social and missionary aims, had, by the end of its first fifteen months, after all the capital outlay had been repaid, only brought in a profit of £25 and even this figure was boosted by a certain amount of concealed underwriting since St. John, to boost its effectiveness, was in the habit of hiring a horse and cart at his own expense to deliver goods to customers.[22] £25 was not going to buy much land. The answer would have to lie in a capital fund which invited contributions from members of the Church and other sympathisers. This took time.

There was also the problem that it was nowhere near as easy as they might have hoped to find land at affordable prices within easy reach. Croydon was, as we have discovered, growing fast, and land prices nearby reflected the potential for even greater expansion.

Kenworthy, meanwhile, was becoming more and more engrossed in wider activities. As his circle of contacts widened, he seems to have grown more and more keen to see the Brotherhood achievements recognised at a national level. In November 1895 he renamed *The Croydon Brotherhood Intelligencer*. It was to become *The New Order*, a title that was not only less parochial, but carried both Biblical and Tolstoyan overtones. "We must", he explained in that edition, "aim to turn ourselves and others from the life of the world and into the 'New Order' of Society which Jesus calls 'The Kingdom of Heaven'". It was, moreover, to be a channel connecting Tolstoy with his English readers; he was 'with us, both in

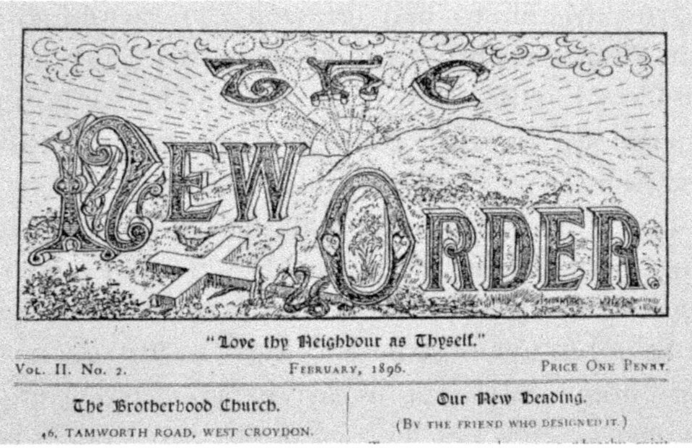

The banner headline of *The New Order*

sympathy and in actual co-operation'.[23] In the *Labour Annual* of 1896 he now openly referred to it as 'the organ in England of the new movement of life and thought which Tolstoy represents'. It was a statement which reflected the degree to which the influence of Tolstoy's thinking had been strengthening within him and the degree to which the Christian Socialist message of the Brotherhood was now being, for him at least, seen as synonymous with and best exemplified in Tolstoy's thoughts. How far he had managed to carry the congregation at the Brotherhood Church in this direction may be reflected in the fact that, when a Swedish visitor who had been with Tolstoy in Russia came to address the Sunday meeting on the writer's character and work, he left with a commission, demonstrated by an eager show of hands, 'to convey the expression of our love to Leo Tolstoy'.[24]

Kenworthy's own relationship to the Russian writer had become much more immediate and personal. Having sent Tolstoy a copy of his *Anatomy of Misery* at the time of publication he had had a reply from the author in March 1894 saying that, not only had he already seen it, but he had arranged for a copy to be translated into Russian. It was, said Kenworthy, the happiest day of his life.[25] Neither let the correspondence lapse and when, in October 1895, Tolstoy wished to get a letter published in *The Times* describing the fate of the persecuted Doukhobor sect in Russia, he chose to send it to Kenworthy, entrusting him with making sure it appeared.[26]

Now, as plans for the colony were advancing, Kenworthy was contemplating nothing less than a pilgrimage to meet the great man himself. Tolstoy, on receiving from Kenworthy several translations from his own works, had written telling him that his friend Vladimir Tchertkoff was also interested in publishing English translations and suggesting they made contact with each other.[27] Tchertkoff wasted no time in writing to Kenworthy to suggest a trip to Russia, promising to meet part of his expenses. Early in 1895 he set off. During his stay in Moscow he met like-minded souls who had, in one way or another, changed the pattern of their lives, many of them now living simply and, as far as possible, self-sufficiently in small dedicated communities. In the depths of the Russian winter he ventured on a 250-mile train and sleigh ride north-east to visit the rural community where Tolstoy's follower (and later biographer) Pavel Biriukoff was attempting to live a life of Tolstoyan Christianity among the peasants on his estate.

Above all, he discussed far into the night matters of belief with the man who, by the end of his visit, he had come to view with nothing short of adulation: "Leo Tolstoy is singled out among men because upon him, at his height, the light of the dawn shines and glows. From him, and those like him, the light creeps down towards the dark places of the earth".[28]

Leo Nikolayevich Tolstoy

These were the terms and this the tone in which, when Kenworthy returned to Croydon, he would have addressed a curious and excited church congregation. *Brotherhood* recorded that his account of his journey 'severely strained the seating capacity of the church'.[29] But if he returned carrying a spiritual torch lit from the flame of the Master's own thoughts and words, he also came bearing news of a practical challenge placed upon Kenworthy's shoulders (and therefore, by implication, on the shoulders of the Brotherhood Church), for Tolstoy had conceded to him the right to publish the first English translations of his hitherto unpublished and all his future works, any profits to be ploughed into the Croydon Brotherhood Publishing Company which would be the medium for publication.[30]

This was a triumph of such a scale that it carried both Kenworthy and the Brotherhood Church over any possible disappointment when, a few months later, in July, Tolstoy wrote stating, in relation to the Church's attempts to found a colony, that he did not believe in communities or brotherhoods establishing themselves as separate groups within society, 'communities of saints amongst sinners' as he described them. It was for the individual to come to his own form of salvation and then to go out into the world to do what he could in support of his fellow man.[31] This aside – and he did put it aside, driven, no doubt, by his firm desire to carry out the social experiment the value of which he had preached so long – Kenworthy returned more determined than ever to devote himself to the spreading of Tolstoy's message and the publishing of his works. The burden of the Church work was now shared with Arthur Baker, a mathematician and a former official in the Indian Civil Service who had given up his career to work with the Salvation Army and had now made the move to the Brotherhood Church.[32]

The search for a colony site continued and, if anything, was stepped up. News was coming in of other attempts to found communities. The March edition of *The New Order* bore a report of the 'Free Communist and Co-operative Colony', set up as a planned 20-acre market garden in the summer of 1895 at Clousden Hill just outside Newcastle by a small group of families determined to live and work by the principles of ethical anarchism. "This is just the sort of effort we are now trying to make at Croydon", commented Kenworthy, pointing out that they had already started 'at the other end of the social structure' by bringing together in Croydon a support mechanism and a market for such a colony.[33] Nearer to home, a member of Wallace's Southgate

Road Brotherhood Church, James Evans, was looking for others to join him in an attempt at communal living on a small cottage plot in Ashingdon in Essex.[34]

Then, at last, a site was located. The hope of finding something within easy striking distance of Croydon had gradually faded and the search had widened. In the end they had lighted upon land on the other side of the capital, in a small Essex village of some 800 inhabitants.[35] Purleigh, the chosen place, was just 35 miles as the crow flies from the centre of London. Kelly's Directory waxed lyrical about its position: "The scenery around it is bold and romantic, the land undulating and from every point there is an extensive view".[36] But it was not in good heart. Depression had been deepening for the better part of twenty years. Just three years before, R. Hunter Pringle, an Assistant Commissioner to the Royal Commission on Agricultural Depression, had visited Purleigh and noted how land that had, twenty years before, been in good shape for growing corn was now uncultivated and left as a sheep-walk. "The buildings are rolling down, the gates are gone and the fences are in deplorable condition".[37] In 1897 the report of a second Commission would describe Essex as, agriculturally, the most depressed county in England and this part of the county, the Dengie peninsula, was generally regarded as the poorest in Essex.[38] Furthermore, it suffered from the lack of any piped water supply, leaving people dependent on often polluted shallow wells and standing ponds, a problem that was already a cause of bitter grievance and would continue to be so for some years to come. People were moving away in search of a better living; the population of Purleigh had shrunk by almost a third in the last fifty years. As a result, land prices were severely depressed.[39]

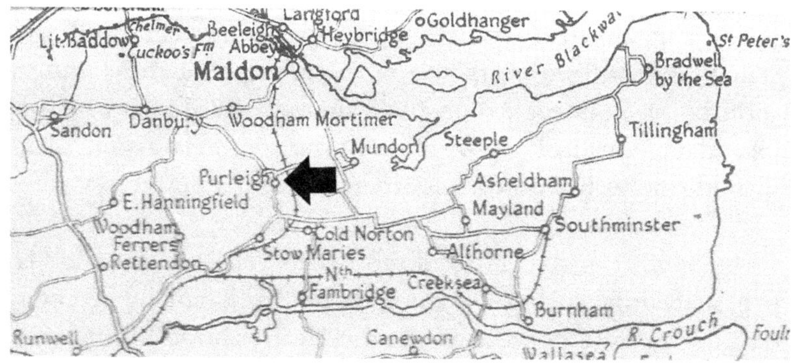

The Dengie Peninsula, Essex

It was this that attracted the Trust to this corner of the country. Here land was going cheap. Mr Joshua Nunn of Hill House in Purleigh, from whom the Brotherhood now proposed to buy ten acres, had acquired part of the 54-acre Avenals Farm back in 1884. Even then the idea of selling off piecemeal was perhaps in his mind. By now he had already sold other plots, as had other local landowners.[40] One ambitious speculator had, in 1891, attempted to divide up nearby land into more than 500 house-sized plots, with new roads, shops and a tavern envisaged to create virtually a new town.[41] It was a pattern that was being repeated across south-east Essex as developers saw an opportunity to buy up unprized agricultural land, divide it into plots and sell it on to would-be house-builders. This was how the sprawling townscape of Southend-on-Sea had come into being.[42] In Purleigh, however, few buyers came forward and the scheme collapsed. Nevertheless, there were always those who were willing to exchange a miserable existence in the worst parts of London for a home in the country, however humble. When, in March 1898, one resident wrote to the local paper complaining of the many ramshackle buildings being put up in the area by Londoners moving out of town, Nunn was quick to reply, pointing out that, while "I could at the present time count over fifty individuals living in my neighbourhood who less than two years ago were residents of the southern suburbs of London", there had already been plenty of old, insanitary, ramshackle properties in the area anyway and locals should not be hard on newcomers seeking a new life.[43]

There can be little doubt that Nunn's interests lay primarily in securing a return on his lands but he seems to have been predisposed towards the Brotherhood Church and its vision of a fair society based on communal effort and communal rewards. A member of a group calling themselves the 'Christian Levellers', he was a frequent contributor to the letters pages of the local press, bemoaning 'these days of insincerity and high notions' and lashing out at 'the jobbery, robbery and snobbery which prevail so luxuriously under a pretence of piety'.[44] His Biblical role model was the Good Samaritan. Bent on practising what he preached, in the October 1896 edition of *The New Order*, 'Comrade Nunn of the Christian Levellers' advertised for fellow-thinkers to join him in a 'Co-operative Land Settlement' near Cold Norton. There is no evidence that it came to pass.

Meanwhile, however, negotiations with Nunn for purchase were underway and by the late summer, the transaction was complete.[45] The Church acquired ten acres at a price of £20 an acre. The original hope, of paying for this new phase of the Brotherhood venture from capital already raised from the Trust's business enterprises, had faded. Instead, and in order to turn the dream into reality without a dispiritingly long delay, a number of the wealthier members of the community made contributions to the purchase price. Many years later, in 1912, William Sinclair would recall that there were nine initial contributors to a fund which included both purchase and initial capital outlay to develop the site.

Kenworthy himself put in £70. Others gave what they could, anything between £10 and £230.[46] But the lion's share came from a lucky windfall, in the shape of church member Arnold Eiloart.

Arnold Eilloart

Eiloart was, one suspects, an enigma to his family. Born into substantial wealth, his father a London solicitor, his mother a novelist, he was set fair for a promising career as an academic chemist. With a degree from the University of London and a doctorate from the University of Leipzig, he had gone off to New York and held academic posts culminating in a professorship at the New York Postgraduate Medical School. He came back to England in 1894 to a lecturing post at the Royal College of Science in South Kensington but he brought back with him evolving ideas on the failings of society and the need for individual self-improvement within it. In New York he had lived in Settlement House, the premises of a newly formed University Settlement Society, established right in the heart of a densely populated and impoverished immigrant area and providing accommodation and educational programmes, mainly for new arrivals to the city. Staffed largely by young graduates, it had become a hot-bed of progressive thinking. Soon after his return to England, Eiloart was to be found living in Lansdowne Road, Croydon and attending the Brotherhood Church where his emerging ideas of social and individual improvement would be regularly fuelled by the speakers who addressed the twice-weekly meetings.

Eiloart's life changed abruptly in April 1895 with the death of his father and his inheritance of a share of the family estate, valued in total at over £11,000. This was just weeks after the first announcement had been made that the Church was seeking land on which to establish its 'Brotherhood Camp'. Eiloart was bent upon placing his money at the disposal of appropriate social causes and the call for funds for land-purchase provided the ideal opportunity. His initial contribution, of £1,650, was the decisive factor. The colony would go ahead.

By September, *The New Order* was inviting readers to apply to the Secretary "to join us, or to help our long-preparing movement 'back to the land'".[47]

Chapter 3

Back to the Land

So it was that our three pioneers found themselves clustered around a cottage fireplace in mid-Essex. They had arrived in the autumn cf 1896 to begin the task of preparing ten acres of arable land ready for planting and to smooth the way for a larger body of colonists who would follow in the spring.

The train that had brought them here soon exchanged the over-populated sprawl of the East End for a rural landscape in visible decline. As they trudged down the lanes from Cold Norton railway station they might have noticed how much of the land seemed neglected.[1] They could not fail to spot the demarcations in some of the nearby fields, subdividing them into small rectangular plots, now being offered for sale for building or for smallholdings.

Cock Clarks as the colonists would have known it

The three-mile walk from the station had brought them to the cottage they had rented to see them through the winter. Cock Clarks was a hamlet of Purleigh, less than half a mile away from the lands they were now to work. A pub, a shop, a blacksmith's forge and a handful of cottages were grouped around a road junction. They would live here until a more permanent arrangement could be arrived at and until then they had set themselves the challenge of living as cheaply as possible – on a maximum of five shillings a week for each of them. But there would be little need beyond food for, while the weather lasted, they would be in the fields for as long as the light allowed them. One later recorded that their diet across this winter consisted of 'cold porridge and an occasional onion to take the taste away'.[2]

South from Cock Clarks, the road towards Stow Maries and Cold Norton – Hackman's Lane – brought them to their 'estate', which lay beside the road, fallow, unworked. They began the task of taking it in hand. The work was hard and repetitive. They dug. They dug day in and day out. The land was a heavy loam. There must have been aches and blisters for these three pioneers had not been born to the labouring life. Two of them, Hubert Hammond and William Sinclair, had been bank clerks; the third, William Sudbury Protheroe, had been intended for his father's auctioneering business in east London. His letter of resignation was, like Hammond's, published in *The New Order*. It began: "The time has come when I must choose between God and Mammon".[3] Only Sinclair, as far as we know, had

William Sudbury ('Sud') Protheroe

had any experience of manual labour. He had, according to Nellie Shaw, later a fellow colonist with him, given up his job with the Bank of Scotland in dissatisfaction with the ethics of the business and attempted to take on a smallholding in Much Hadham, Hertfordshire, which he was to work with a fellow-thinker. When this fell through, he had heard of and applied to join the Purleigh experiment.[4]

For all of them this was a gamble which they were taking out of a conviction that there had to be another way, a better way. Each of them had invested in the project according to his means: Protheroe £10, Hammond £70 and Sinclair £180, sums which went into the wider General Fund both for the initial purchase of land and to sustain the project until the day it might become self-supporting.[5] Now their labour across this winter was to provide the foundation upon which the colony would be built.

The men were not entirely alone over the winter. By February two more had come to join them and there were also occasional visitors from Croydon, curious to see the spot where the future lay. Most useful to them was William Hone, now in his forties, the son of a Warwickshire farmer and a gardener all his adult life. Living in Benson Road, Croydon with his wife and four children, he had been drawn into the life of the Brotherhood Church and had now been persuaded to give advice to the novice smallholders on horticultural matters, advice which was to prove indispensable over the next few years.

With Hone's help, by the time spring finally made its appearance the three men could look out across three acres of land, all turned over by spadework and ready for planting. Half an acre had been dug deep - down to a depth of three feet – with a view to creating an orchard. It was a brave start. And now others followed. By April a local paper was able to report about half a dozen colonists in residence, among them, on a more permanent basis, Hone, his wife and three children. They had been offered a pound a week to move to Purleigh by Eiloart (who also came in the spring) and they arrived – along with six fowls and two goats – in a pantechnicon, dragged with difficulty along the deep mud of country roads after torrential April rain.[6] They set up home in a house half a mile away from the colony, the nearest that could for the moment be found, but they settled in, in what Hammond described as 'their own cheery work-a-way style'.

By April 1897 there was a mood of springtime optimism at the colony. Hubert Hammond had now taken on the role of Purleigh correspondent for the Brotherhood Church's monthly newspaper *The New Order* and in that month's issue he was able to report that a good deal of planting had now been done in the newly dug ground and a wire fence put around the land to keep off the sheep and cattle which passed along the road on their way to market. A tool-shed had been built and a workshop, ten feet by twenty, was nearing completion, while they were now building a greenhouse, intended eventually to be a hundred feet long and partially heated. A swarm of bees had been acquired and three hen-houses had been put up, stocked already with forty birds and with more than a hundred eggs in an incubator made by William Sinclair the previous autumn. By May *The New Order* would be able to advertise 'daily supplies of new laid eggs from Purleigh Colony'.[7] This was a small but significant moment, the first evidence that the long-held dream of linking the produce of the land to workers in the town in a co-operative bond might become a reality.

It goes without saying that it had not taken long for the locals to become interested in what was going on at Avenals. They could scarcely have failed to notice the new arrivals:

The majority of the colonists went without hats, and many of them wore neither shoes nor stockings, and the women wore very short skirts. Some of the men wore their hair long, and if it were a windy day they would tie it back with a ribbon.[8]

Late in March a reporter turned up from the *Essex County Chronicle*.[9] One of the colonists – there is no record of his name – was allocated to show him around and explain the purpose behind their endeavours. The result, as it appeared in the *Chronicle* of 2 April, under the headline ' "Bread Labour" at Purleigh' did its best to make sense of the notes made by the reporter as he struggled to grasp the explanation given to him:

The principle at the basis of the undertaking is to substitute, as far as that may be done, co-operation for competition. The colonist reasons thus in favour of 'bread-labour'. A man draws his whole living from the producers of necessaries. If, however, you produce a picture or I produce a book, these are not absolute necessaries of life. Mankind might exist without books or pictures – though happily man does not so exist – but without food existence would be impossible. What I say then is that if you make a man exchange the food which he produces out of the earth for the book I have written, you are doing something unjust to him. It is not an equal bargain. Broadly stated, the aim at Purleigh will be to grow as much food as possible – meaning vegetables, fruit and so on. Anything we do not need for our own sustenance can be sold against the provision of clothes and other necessaries which we cannot provide from the land.

There is a mixture of ideas here, but at the heart of it (the clue is in the title to the article which clearly came from the colonist-informant) is an important and, for the colony, influential theory, that of 'Bread Labour'. The dignity of manual labour was a theme which had a long history and many of the colonists would have found it in the writings of John Ruskin. But the concept of 'bread labour' was more specific. It was that every man and woman, regardless of wealth or rank, should contribute sufficient manual labour to produce the food needed to sustain themselves and that if everyone lived by this creed, social distinctions and competition would disappear and harmony reign. This had been enunciated by the Russian peasant-writer T. M. Bondarev and was enthusiastically adopted by Tolstoy in his own *What Then Must We Do?*, one of the texts which inspired Kenworthy. Indeed one wonders whether it was Kenworthy himself who had met and enlightened the reporter as best he could in Tolstoyan thought.

Back in Croydon, with regular reports arriving of developments at Purleigh, excitement mounted at the prospect of achieving this next stage in the grand design. Looking back in her memoir, written in 1935, Nellie Shaw recalled: "It makes one smile, but in those days [the spring of 1897] it looked to some of us as if, to gain salvation, one must join the Colony".[10] Hone's arrival had brought solid experience and down-to-earth practicality and things moved ahead rapidly. Hammond's 'Purleigh Notes' in *The New Order* painted a picture of a developing agricultural paradise, a cornucopia of harvests to come.

By June a third of the massive greenhouse had been completed, fitted with a boiler for heating and planted out with tomatoes and vines. There was disappointment when the newly completed incubator failed to do its job and most of the eggs refused to hatch but this was remedied. Half an acre of double-dug land was planted with potatoes, in part for food and in part to help clean and improve the rather poor land. Vegetables and grain were sown, not only to supplement those being grown by the colonists in the gardens of their rented cottages, but also to see for future years what did best and what would not work here. French beans, haricots and runners did well and would provide seed for the spring. Sunflowers would provide food for the poultry. Corn looked promising, there was a good crop of peas in August and the heated greenhouse produced a fine crop of tomatoes, though those grown outside were much less successful. A six-acre meadow was prepared, ready to produce the colony's first crop of hay.

Many of the colonists were vegetarians and dairying was important. By the end of the year, the goats were providing milk, the chickens were laying well and the colony's two cows, secured in exchange for the promise of future dairy produce, were installed in a cowshed big enough eventually to house six.

Meanwhile, attention had also turned to the problem of providing housing on-site for the colonists, who, up until now, had been living in rented accommodation; by May they were scattered among four cottages. Here luck was on their side. Most of the surrounding countryside sat on heavy clay but the colony site happened to be in a small pocket of brick-earth which surrounded the hamlet of Cock Clarks.[11] Determined on the path of self-sufficiency, training was sought from an experienced brickmaker and some of the colonists, in particular William Sinclair and Arthur Drover, were set the task of digging out brick-earth from a pit on part of the site.[12] This was work which, to those accustomed to more sedentary ways of life, would test anyone's commitment. Hammond wrote with feeling when he recorded in the columns of *The New Order* the difficulty of getting up early on chilly mornings to go out into the field to tread the clay to make it workable. It was slow work but by September three batches of bricks – some 7,000 – had been produced and the reward for all this labour took the shape of the completed walls of a six-room brick cottage standing there for all to see and for some – eventually – to live in. There were even enough bricks left over to be stored against the day when they would build a barn.

By November a local reporter, shown around by Mr Nunn, painted an admiring portrait of what had been achieved:

Bundles of young trees lay about awaiting planting. Patches of wheat and oat stubble and patches of standing maize gave evidence of experiments in agriculture. A forest of sunflowers, originally intended for the manufacture of oil, is now intended to supply the poultry with food during the winter… The potato patches have yielded a goodly store, which is clamped in the open, and carrots and beetroot are being treated in like manner. Savoys and other green stuff are grown, while in a long greenhouse there is a gay array of ripening tomatoes.[13]

Satisfying as this harvest must have seemed, it had been won the hard way. It had been a year of learning. Each stage of activity produced, it seemed, another problem to be solved. Building and brickmaking demanded an enormous and un-predicted amount of water, all of which had to be shipped to the brick-earth from the only pond on the farm by means of a 180-foot long shute. By the end of the summer the pond was virtually empty. The decision was made to turn the situation to advantage. The rest of the water was pumped out and a hundred tons of rich black mud was systematically dug out, to be used in the following year as a fertiliser on what they had already discovered to be pretty poor land. By increasing the depth of the pond it was hoped to solve the problem of water shortage.[14] It was only a limited success; by the following September the colony was again without water and was forced to fetch supplies from further afield.[15]

Indispensable in all of this were the horse (called Johnny, he had previously pulled a London bus), a cart, which proved an essential purchase for shifting clay, mud and manure and other materials, and the pony and cart which had been contributed by 'a friend of the Colony' in exchange for future services.[15] This carried not only colonists and visitors but, more valuably, produce from the farm, to the nearest large town, Maldon (five miles away) or to the railway station, from where it was taken to supply the Brotherhood shops, both in Croydon and in Hackney. By the end of the summer this was happening and the prospect of united co-operative producers and outlets was turning into a reality.

At the end of 1897 there were, according to *The New Order*, fifteen colonists living permanently on-site and about 35 people who had come to Essex 'with some desire to live worthy lives'. When a local reporter descended on them in

November he found a group taking their lunch break in the as yet incomplete brick house.

> Entering, we found some eight or nine men and youths just finishing their frugal midday meal of vegetarian diet.[17] Their soiled faces, hands and clothing did not hide their intellectual culture and manly bearing. Devoid of all stiff, conventional behaviour, they appeared to be a happy-go-lucky set of fellows, enjoying themselves intensely in their simple way. They were grouped on a couple of extemporised seats, made of planks and bricks in a room which had just been plastered.[18]

We know some but not all of the names of the fifteen 'core colonists' at this time. Many came from Croydon. There was Herbert Archer, barely in his twenties when he came to Purleigh, a former clerk in an insurance office who had become the Brotherhood Church Secretary the year before. Of the same age was Arthur Drover, a tailor's apprentice when he had joined the Brotherhood in Croydon. Along with William MacDonald, he had run a tailoring and bootmaking business for the Trust. These joined the 'pioneers' and others followed over the next few years.

Among the colonists and those living in the neighbourhood who joined in the work and aims of the colony were a number of women. Salome Fifield, an occasional visitor, speaks of six, other than herself. We could name Charlotte ('Lottie') Dunn, Lois Hone and her teenage daughter Maud, Georgina ('Ina') Hopwood, Nellie Shaw and Jeannie Straughan as being present in Purleigh for varying lengths of time. There would no doubt have been more casual visitors. Fifield's account of colony life emphasises that the women played their part in digging and planting and other horticultural chores but it also makes clear that, even in this progressive community, the traditional 'womanly chores' of cleaning, washing and cooking were accepted as their primary duties.[19]

It was by no means a static group at the colony and there were always a substantial number of people on the fringes, not ready or able to commit to working and living on the holding but interested enough to come and stay for varying lengths of time in the neighbourhood. Some from Croydon seem to have regarded the colony in the way Kenworthy had described it before the land had been found: "a piece of land … where we can pitch 'Brotherhood Camp' and … during the summer, inaugurate our longed-for exodus … by days and afternoons of holiday-making upon our own acres".[20] *The New Order* was used as a means of advertising this possibility to sympathetically minded thinkers; a 'Brotherhood Colonies Agency', operating out of the Paternoster Square office of the Publishing Company, as well as offering fresh eggs from the colony, highlighted, under the heading 'Summer Holidays at Reasonable Rates', the availability of "holiday facilities on the Purleigh Colony. Sympathisers are invited to get some fresh air into their lungs free of charge by working on the land. Implements provided free, and they can work as hard as they like. All they have to pay for is food and lodging".[21]

Visitors from Croydon kept alive the excitement of the experiment. Some, like Nellie Shaw, felt unable to give up their current commitments, in her case the running of the Croydon dressmaking business. Her life would later be lived out in a colony, but that time had not yet come and for the moment she was a sporadic visitor, returning home, as did others, with stories of how the future was shaping out in Purleigh.

Not every visitor was as engaged or supportive, however. Reactions were mixed.

> Lots of them come to see us as they would go to see a menagerie, and seem rather surprised and disappointed to find us so much like other people. One woman was heard to say to another, "Why, they speak quite like ladies." Then again there are those who come with a view to joining us, but after a week or two many of them find the life too hard or too monotonous, and return to the towns. But they generally remain more or less in sympathy with us, and many of them send us parcels of groceries or bundles of clothes when they can afford it.[22]

Salome Hocking Fifield, Authoress

These words were put into the mouth of a fictional Purleigh colonist by another 'semi-detached' arrival, Salome Fifield, who came with her husband Arthur, a publisher, whom she had married in 1894. Both members of the Croydon church (Arthur was Secretary for a while), they had been slowly drawn into an involvement with Vladimir Tchertkoff's publishing aspirations and visited Purleigh from time to time. Salome, already a published novelist under her maiden name, Salome Hocking, would wait until 1905 before she published (through her husband's own company) *Belinda the Backward: a Romance of Modern Idealism*, a fictionalised but vivid picture of colony life.[23] Though it would be unwise to place too much weight on the individual episodes and characters in her book, nothing captures so completely the spirit and ambitions, the arduous work and the sheer enthusiasm of the group at the time.

Chapter 4

DISTRACTIONS

Shaw's recollection of feeling impelled at this time to join the colony in order 'to gain salvation' is an indicator of a shift taking place in Croydon during 1897. The reports from the burgeoning colony at Purleigh were reinforced in *The New Order* by a new series of articles, gathered together by Arthur Baker, recording similar experiments in communal living, not only in Britain but around the world, among them the long-standing Topolobampo Bay Colony in Mexico, the Cosme Colony in Paraguay and an Italian Anarchist-Communist colony in Brazil. The fact that all these were having problems did not take away from the sense imparted, that Purleigh was part of a worldwide movement. Moreover, the inclusion of all these reports tended to squeeze news of activities in Croydon into a smaller area of print and it is not perhaps fanciful to see this as a gradual shifting of emphasis away from what were now up-and-running local enterprises towards the excitement of the newly blossoming Purleigh experiment. The tail was beginning to wag the dog.

A more surprising change was the decision, announced in the October issue of *The New Order*, to drop the name 'Brotherhood Church'. Kenworthy's explanation seems curiously thin:

> As some (however slight) approximation to the living practice of our principle has been made, it has been felt that the facts of what we say and do are best left to speak for themselves, and we may dispense with names as we do with creeds. … When the new spirit moves in men, perforce they burst the old bonds of names, creeds and institutions, and seek for new, vital, intimate embodiments of their spirit.[1]

Thereafter Kenworthy no longer described himself as 'pastor' and the Sunday sessions were simply described in *The New Order* as 'Croydon Meetings'.

Was it a coincidence that in small print, in the same edition, a notice appeared advising readers that 'J.C. Kenworthy wishes to make known that after 1st Oct. his address will be Hill Farm, Woodham Ferris, nr. Chelmsford, Essex'? It was the next parish to Purleigh. Certainly it would seem that the centre of his attention was shifting.

Kenworthy was now more and more deeply involved up and down the country in writing, speaking and sitting on the committees of progressive bodies. Throughout these years the pace of his writing and publishing had steadily increased. He had followed up *The Anatomy of Misery* with a volume of broadly Christian Socialist essays and addresses, *Christian Revolt*, and then, in 1894, with *From Bondage to Brotherhood: an Address to the Workers*, a strongly worded call to the working men of England to reject and ignore the power of the establishment and instead to pursue the route of self-improvement and communal action. The influence of Tolstoy is unmistakeable. The doctrine is what would come to be described as ethical anarchism. It is the tone of this book that surprises. It reminds us how forceful Kenworthy had become in his beliefs and how compelling an orator and writer he now was:

The Law has been framed by oppressors; neglect it, let it die. In place of it, by the power of Brotherhood will come up the true Democratic means of Government - unfettered Public Opinion which is the Will of the People. Keep away from lawyers, judges; on your parts, let the Law perish. But give heed to those who tell you that the first change needed is in your own hearts, in your own ways of looking upon life and upon each other; who can help to marshal you in industrial regiments, and show you the peaceful way to win back all whereof you have been robbed. Those who understand the power of the commercial machinery, know, past doubt, that if you workers so willed, the General Strike and General Cooperation would gain England for you in a week, and turn it into Paradise in a twelvemonth.

In July 1896 Kenworthy addressed the International Socialist Workers and Trade Union Congress, repeating his view that 'the English nation is ready to give up politics as a weapon and turn to industrial co-operation on free Anarchist Communist principles'.[2] This was to prove a famously divisive conference from which the anarchists would be essentially driven out by the Marxist communists, widening a breach which would prove irreversible. The anarchists then met separately in a club in Frith Street Soho to discuss the future and among the leading figures from Britain and Europe who addressed that meeting - they included Errico Malatesta, Louise Michel, veteran of the Paris Commune and Peter Kropotkin - was John Kenworthy, essentially holding the torch for Tolstoy's particular brand of Christian anarchism.

It may be useful, at this point, to pause and consider what the word anarchism meant for the public at large in the 1890s. Then, as now, it would most immediately have conjured up the image of shadowy, ruthless, bomb-throwing individuals who would stop at nothing to overthrow governments: terrorists, as we would now call them. Indeed, the image would have been even sharper at the time than now, for anarchist bombs and murders - and rumours of them - were widespread across Europe. In England an anarchist had blown himself up in an explosion in Greenwich Park in 1894 and a spate of bomb attacks on London post offices had followed.[3]

1897 would see a lethal explosion on a London underground train. The newspapers portrayed this as an ever-present terrorist threat. No matter that Kenworthy, Tolstoy and many others stood for a totally different type of anarchism: for a denial of governmental and other forms of imposed authority certainly, but for their gradual and peaceful replacement by moral and co-operative codes of personal behaviour and social interaction. This very marked distinction would have been lost on the public at large, not perhaps surprisingly when these two wings of the anarchist movement were often to be found speaking at the same meetings. In August 1896, for example, Kenworthy addressed a meeting in Trafalgar Square demanding the release of the 'Walsall Anarchists' who had been imprisoned in 1892 for allegedly planning explosions, charges which were (and are) widely seen as having been orchestrated by the Metropolitan Police Special Branch. The easy confusion in the minds of the world at large would at times have an effect upon the way events at Purleigh would be painted and interpreted.

'An Anarchist Arrested', a French cartoon of 1892

Meanwhile Kenworthy's frequent 'missionary' travels around the country had led to a new 'Brotherhood shoot' springing up. 1897 was marked across the country by a wave of strikes in the engineering sector. In Leeds matters had got very bitter, with lock-outs, blacklisting of suspected agitators and police detectives used to gather evidence of intimidation amongst strikers. Resulting prosecutions only heightened the tensions. It was chance which brought Kenworthy here at this time to preach his doctrine of ethical Tolstoyan anarchism. This in turn led to the formation of a Leeds Brotherhood Church.[4]

Spurred on by a campaigning Socialist Methodist preacher, D. B. Foster, Albert Gibson, an electrician with sympathy for both the strikers' cause and Kenworthy's views, married the two together by offering his workshop at 6 Victoria Street as the base for a workers' collective for the repair of electrical goods and the manufacture of bicycles, as well as a meeting place for the Brotherhood Church.[5] To Kenworthy this must have seemed all too welcome evidence that the Brotherhood message was beginning to be heard beyond Croydon and Purleigh. He would, as the year progressed, dedicate more and more time to the incipient group, spending whole weeks in Leeds to preach, teach and encourage through practical activity.

Alongside all this intensive political activism and his work in Croydon (he was still regularly addressing the Sunday meetings), he was somehow managing to honour the commitment given to Tolstoy in Russia early in 1896 to publish and disseminate his writings in Britain. Already, by the end of 1895, the newly established Brotherhood Publishing Company had advertised for sale *What I Believe, Work While Ye Have the Light* and the first part of *The Four Gospels*

Harmonised and Translated, all by Tolstoy, as well as Kenworthy's writings to date. On his return from Russia, by working with a Russian translator friend, Sid Rapoport, he had, within months, published Tolstoy's story *Master and Man*. Within the year he would publish another of his stories, *Boyhood*, and his essay *Christ's Christianity*, as well as Kenworthy's own account of his visit to Russia, *A Pilgrimage to Tolstoy* and a semi-autobiographical story of his own, *The World's Last Passage*.

Small wonder then that he found it difficult, while preaching the doctrine of Tolstoyan anarchism, to participate fully in the experiment he had himself set running in Essex to secure a better future for society, a future lived on Tolstoyan lines. It was not for any failure of belief. On the contrary, ever since he had visited the great man, his involvement with the charismatic Tolstoy was becoming ever deeper and more committed. That involvement was now going to tie the future and to some extent the fate of the Purleigh colony to events then happening some 2,000 miles away in a remote part of the Caucasian mountains in what is now Georgia, close to the Turkish border.

The letter Tolstoy had asked Kenworthy to get published in *The Times* back in October 1895 (before his visit to the master in Russia) had been intended to draw to the world's attention the fate of the Doukhobors, a religious sect in whose long-held beliefs Tolstoy had found remarkable similarities to what he himself had come to think and promulgate. For the Doukhobors, the spirit of God lived in each man and woman and it was for each and every human to discover and respect this in themselves, to live simply, in peace with others, free of all churches, rituals and priests and, above all, rejecting all human authority, including the rule of law and of government, on the grounds that they constituted a form of oppression or violence. They had now come into conflict with the Tsarist authorities over the issue of military conscription, an accepted norm in Russia at times of crisis or need. In June 1895 a group of Doukhobors had publicly burned their arms in defiance of this requirement and the results had been immediate and vicious. Cossack soldiers had been sent in to their Caucasian villages, there had been beatings and despoliation and some 450 Doukhobor families had been driven out of their settled homes and forced into exile in the malarial valleys of Georgia where many died. Alongside the letter came a detailed eye-witness account of these atrocities, provided to Tolstoy by his friend, Pavel Biriukoff.

The letter did not have the immediate effect of stirring up British public opinion as Tolstoy had hoped. *The Times* editorial in the same issue took the view that the Doukhobors had none but themselves to blame for putting their religious beliefs above obedience to the rule of law. But Tolstoy was undaunted and, when Kenworthy visited him a few months later, the subject was prominent among those discussed.

Doukhobor women in traditional costume pulling a plough

The cause was now taken up by Tolstoy's friend, confidant and right-hand man, Vladimir Tchertkoff, an aristocrat and childhood friend of Tsar Alexander III who, moved by a spirit of Christian liberalism, had resigned his army commission in 1879 to devote himself to the education of the serfs on his estate and had thus drawn close to Tolstoy. Shocked by the attacks on the Doukhobors, Tchertkoff now devoted himself to collecting accounts of the history and recent treatment of the sect, notes which he would bring together in a pamphlet which, together with two Tolstoyan colleagues, Biriukoff and Ivan Treguboff, he published in December 1896 under the title *Pogomite (Help!)*, drawing down the inevitable and immediate wrath of the authorities. In February, Tchertkoff's St. Petersburg apartment was searched and he was told he was likely to be sent into exile, almost certainly to Siberia. In the event, through direct intervention from the Tsar, he was given the option of serving his period of banishment in England, a country he knew well from family visits as a child and from the English tutors and nannies of his early years. Within weeks he had left Russia with his family, a housekeeper, a maid and some friends.

It was at Tchertkoff's suggestion that Kenworthy had visited Tolstoy in Moscow and he had acted as his host during the visit. Kenworthy already regarded him as a friend and it was scarcely surprising that, as soon as he arrived in England in the spring of 1897, Tchertkoff made his way to Croydon, taking a large property called Broomfield House on Duppas Hill, close to Brotherhood House. Within months, Kenworthy's recently established Brotherhood Publishing Company had issued an extended English language version of *Pogomite* under the title *Christian Martyrdom in Russia* with a preface by Kenworthy, a prefatory note by Tchertkoff (addressed from 'Broomfield'), and an afterword by Tolstoy himself.[6] Contributions to a relief fund were to be sent to Tchertkoff in Croydon.

Vladimir Gregorovitch Tchertkoff,
painted by Ilya Repin, c.1890

Aylmer and Louise Maude

Another arrival in Croydon from Russia was the 39-year old former Director of the Anglo-Russian Carpet Company, Aylmer Maude, who appeared with his wife, Louise, and four small boys. The son of an Ipswich clergyman, Maude had been in Russia since he was sixteen, teaching and then working in the carpet business, where he had made enough money to retire before he was forty. He had met Tolstoy in 1888 and became a frequent visitor to Yasnaya Polyana, 'almost every week' in the years leading up to his return to England.[7] Kenworthy had met him on his trip to Moscow in the winter of 1895/6 and they had together had discussions with Tolstoy. Through Tchertkoff, Maude had been swept up in the campaign on behalf of the Doukhobors. He and his wife had found themselves secretly printing illicit copies of an appeal for funds in support of the cause.[8]

Like Tchertkoff, his arrival in England saw him bent on forwarding Tolstoy's interests and, most immediately, widening support for the beleaguered Doukhobors. An intensity of purpose was building on Duppas Hill. But though both men engaged to some degree with the Brotherhood Church while in Croydon, they soon came to realise that the core energy of the group had now shifted more than fifty miles away, to Purleigh. They both quickly followed.

Tchertkoff took a substantial 18th-century miller's house about a mile away from the colony, in Mill Lane, close to the centre of Purleigh village. Maude set up his family to the west of the colony, half a mile away across the fields, in Wickham's Farm, just on the parish boundary with neighbouring Woodham Ferrers. Both men seem to have integrated well with the colonists and both were made honorary members of the colony, entitled to sit in on and participate in the weekly meetings which were now part of the life of the colony. When yet another local reporter came around in August 1898, he

Mill House, Tchertkoff's residence in Purleigh

Wickham's Farm, home to the Maudes

found Tchertkoff and his wife cooking up a vegetarian meal for the colonists.[9] Maude and his wife in particular threw themselves actively into the life of the colony. Their house became a regular meeting place, with occasional musical soirées and spare rooms used to put up visitors. Every day two of the colonists would be invited to dine with the family and Louise's kitchen skills were constantly at the service of the colony, cooking mid-day meals in an open-air communal kitchen set up under an awning. One of the colonists, Sudbury Protheroe, used the brick oven in the kitchen at Wickham's to bake bread for them all, having learned the skill from Mrs Hone.[10] But their commitment was also a financial one. Maude contributed £230 to the communal fund, as well as a pair of cows which supplied the colony's butter.

To those colonists for whom Tolstoy provided a keystone in their search for a better life – and we should certainly not make the mistake of believing that that was by any means all of them; motives and motivation were mixed – the presence at Purleigh of Maude, Tchertkoff and (from time to time) Kenworthy, all of them now personally associated with and in touch with the great man, must have seemed like a hotline to Yasnaya Polyana and a wholehearted affirmation of the importance of the project and their labour. We know that Tchertkoff and Maude were writing regularly to Tolstoy during this time and news would have passed back and forth.[11] A regular subject would have been the Doukhobors, the immediate reason for Tchertkoff's exile to England.

A major reason for publishing *Christian Martyrdom in Russia* had been to gather financial support for the Doukhobors, many of whom were at risk now of starvation. Raising funds proved not too difficult, especially when the Society of Friends joined in the campaign. But delivering financial help to the Doukhobors in the teeth of the Russian government's clear and manifest oppression seemed a more intractable problem. The only possibility appeared to be to send someone to Georgia with the funds and to deliver them directly into the hands of those who were suffering. Cometh the hour, cometh the man, in the shape of the redoubtable Arthur St. John, the ex-army officer who had been converted to Tolstoy's ideas while reading *The Kingdom of God is Within You*. On his return to England from duty in Burma, he had joined the Croydon Brotherhood and proved invaluable as store manager, organiser of soup kitchens and exercise classes for boys and girls in Croydon and then as emissary to Starnthwaite to learn about the running of colonies. St. John had corresponded with Tolstoy in the past and would remain in touch with him for years to come. He now set off, travelling first to Yasnaya Polyana, where Tolstoy provided him with a letter of introduction to the Doukhobors. It was January 1898 before he finally made contact with them in the Caucasus and was able to hand over the money and get first-hand news of their plight. It would be some time, however, before he could return home. He was now arrested and expelled to Turkey from where he had to find his way back to England.

There is every reason to suppose that the colonists at Purleigh were caught up, both in the pressure to contribute finance to this cause (those who were in any position to do so) and in the general distraction caused by what was essentially an international campaign being conducted on their doorstep. As 1898 developed, this complication would become a substantial issue, but for now the work of the colony had to go on.

Chapter 5

A Canal to the Kingdom of Heaven

Just before Christmas 1897 Hone and his family had taken up residence in the newly-built brick house which had taken so much labour to produce. Given that the colonists had only started digging clay in May and that building had started in August, with help from a sympathetic bricklayer from Maylandsea, it was a significant climax to a busy and productive year. It was also a milestone, celebrated at a house-warming party with singing, dancing and recitations.[1] Whatever 1898 might bring, there was every reason to look back with real satisfaction on the achievements visible all around them. And those achievements were being watched and noted across the country. The regular reports in *The New Order* were in turn picked up in other progressive journals of the time. People with similar ambitions and interests came to see how the colony was working; in October Hammond recorded one visitor from a colony in the north of the country and another from the west who was contemplating starting just such a venture. There was also a gradual accretion of fresh candidates for the new life now being built here in Essex. The core of colonists able to live on-site remained fairly steady at around 15 but others came and lived nearby in order to share the experience of life and work at Purleigh. By October they had actually had to put off new would-be joiners for want of adequate resources and facilities. When the 1898 edition of the *Labour Annual* was published it spoke of no less than 65 colonists. Each new arrival came with a slightly different set of hopes and expectations. And as the numbers grew the business of welding them together into a cohesive and harmonious whole became more important and more difficult.

By now a weekly business meeting had been instituted, to which all colonists were invited. Here the business affairs of the colony were discussed and plans made for future programmes of work. Decision-making was collective, requiring unanimity of view among the gathered colonists. Once the business was done, everyone drank tea and gave themselves over to an evening of music or readings or discussion.[2] There was another get-together on Sunday afternoons, very much on the lines of the Croydon Social Questions Conferences, when, as Hubert Hammond reported:

> Most of us (the colonists and those connected with the colony) meet together … in the hope of getting spiritual help from one another. By this I mean bringing an open mind to the consideration of any subject that may be read or talked about and stating one's best thoughts on the matter. There is no fixed form of proceedings and anyone who cares to come is welcomed to these meetings. Very often Labour Church songs are sung, and the evening is spent in a more or less serious discussion, or music, or both.[3]

These Sunday meetings, at which there was no chairman and individuals were invited to preside for the occasion, must have served as bonding sessions for the colonists, reaffirming their common roots in the Brotherhood Church and their shared interests in the very questions of personal conduct and social improvement which had brought them here. That the sense of development, both collective and personal, was strengthening is also suggested by the provision of classes, among them one in agriculture and another a reading group, which spent the winter of 1897 reading and discussing Shakespeare's plays.[4]

There were moments of intense harmony. Early in July 1898, to mark the completion of haymaking, the colonists took themselves off on a celebratory excursion. They walked en masse the five miles to the village of Little Baddow, to a spot on the river Chelmer where they bathed, ate their picnic and listened to a lecture by one of their number before taking tea at the nearby 'Rodney' inn. 'The walk back in the cool of the evening concluded a pleasant day of restful recreation'.[5]

In the event and with the benefit of historical hindsight, this moment might be seen as something of an apex for the dream of community. By the end of the month things would have changed, subtly but irrevocably. But at that moment everything seemed, on the surface at least, to be going well. The workforce was growing, under Hone's guidance the horticulture and agriculture were thriving as the hard preparatory work gave way to a more manageable seasonal pattern of labour and the colony was being accepted as part of the Purleigh landscape. It seems clear that the colonists worked hard to ensure good relations with the locals, in whom the arrival of this rather exotic group must have initially aroused suspicions. Other rural colonies of the same period often inspired rumours of immoral practices and, amid press hysteria about bomb-throwing anarchists, of dark and doubtful intentions. Purleigh might equally have been prone to just such concerns. The memory was still fresh of the murder of a local police sergeant in 1893, found in a ditch in the village, bludgeoned and with his throat cut.[6] Then, in July 1897, 'a drunken brawl among six peapickers of the tramp class', as the rector described them, had ended in a 'murderous assault' on P.C. Giggins, the local bobby.[7] In a small and fairly remote village these were major events and the temptation to blame 'foreigners' must have been irresistible.

Doubts and rumours would no doubt have multiplied in the parish, especially with the arrival from Croydon of Tchertkoff's Russian entourage, which included no less than a princess. The *Manchester Guardian* reporter had spoken of the villagers' 'native stolidity' having been 'considerably shaken by these strange settlers in their midst'. Nevertheless, he pointed out, the colonists were at pains to dispel these fears, giving free entertainments to the villagers to the accompaniment of a convenient piano in one of their cottages.[8] In August, the colonists borrowed a barn from a local farmer and put on a programme of songs and sketches for the locals. Over a hundred turned up. The following day they were invited to join in what was an echo of the regular Sunday meetings in Croydon and a curious audience of eighty came along. There were Labour Church hymns, readings of a socialist leaning, including William Morris's 'Dream of John Bull', an address by Arthur St. John and some comic songs to round things off.

If there was a degree of proselytising intended by this engagement, it was applied with the lightest of touches, as Hammond explained:

> There is very little to amuse the people here, and it is a great pleasure to us to be able to introduce a little brightness into their lives. We do not desire to press our views on anyone, but to seek out for ourselves the source of true life and earnestly strive to live this life; and we desire that others may do the same, not necessarily in the same way that we have adopted, but intelligently and conscientiously working out their own salvation.[9]

This was by no means the last attempt at outreach. On 18 February 1898 Miss Pilch, the mistress at the local school, recorded in the log book that "an entertainment was given this evening in this school-room by Mr Burtt, a friend of the colonists, assisted by the colonists themselves. It was very good indeed. The room was packed with people".[10]

When term started again, in September, the good relations were further cemented when "Miss Eleanor [blank], a Russian lady, visited at 9 a.m. and stayed until 12 a.m. to see the routine of an English Village School". This was almost certainly Princess Elena Petrovna who had come to Croydon, complete with entourage, to join Tchertkoff's party-in-exile and had then followed on to Purleigh.

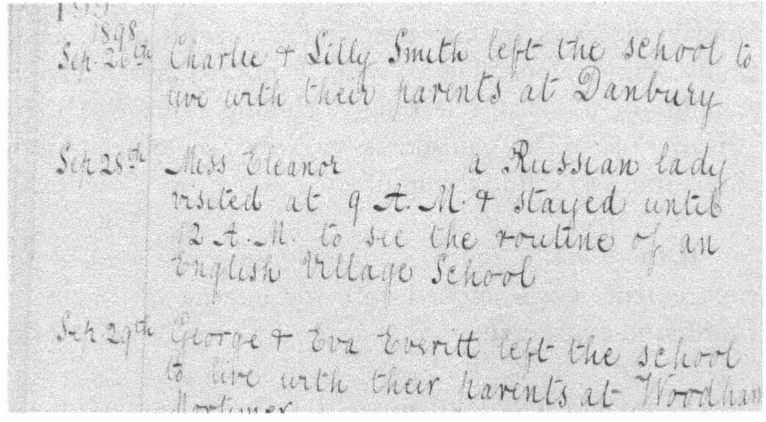

Miss Pilch's record of the Russian visitor to the school

Interest in the colony was not simply local. Even though it was far from paying its way as yet, so much had confidence in its future grown that in the spring of 1898 a further thirteen acres were acquired, more than doubling the size of the initial plot at Purleigh.[11] Kenworthy seized this golden moment to draw the attention of the wider world to what had been achieved by brotherhood and co-operation. During August a succession of journalists found their way to Purleigh, leading Hammond to complain that the month had been marked by "excessive heat, and a plague of wasps, journalists, visitors and sympathisers".[12]

The *Clarion*, which sent a reporter down from its offices in Manchester, was a socialist newspaper, founded in 1891 by Robert Blatchford, the author of the influential *Merrie England*. This was a newspaper well disposed to what was being attempted in Purleigh and when the report appeared it spoke of the colony as 'an attempt to cut a Suez Canal to the Kingdom of Heaven'. The colonists had, it claimed, 'jumped the chasm from competition to Co-operation without waiting for the plank of social democracy and have arrived on the shores of anarchism'.[13]

Others were less sympathetic. The *Daily News*, a national paper with a track-record of progressive, sometimes radical thought, spoke first to Tchertkoff and praised his work and sacrifices in Russia on behalf of the Doukhobors, but when their reporter was shown around the colony by Hubert Hammond he became critical to the point of sarcasm:

Some of Tolstoy's English disciples also live at Purleigh. They are trying to get "off the backs of the people". A satisfying explanation of this phrase I cannot give. I merely know that if the gentle reader would have the goodness "to get off my back and I off the gentle reader's, and all other persons off one another's, then – in the Tolstoy view – everybody would have plenty to eat and drink, adequate lodging and leisure, and, in fact, opportunity for a high old time. The way to bring this condition about, it would appear, is to get a bit of land and dig it for all you are worth; then cultivate goose-berries and grass, wheat and watercress, plums and potatoes, and other toothsome things; build yourself a habitation with home-made bricks; run up a greenhouse for the rearing of tomatoes; keep two cows and a calf, a horse and a pony, several hives of bees, a disreputable-looking old goat, and the usual rabble of restless cocks and hens. Those things the eighteen colonists of Purleigh have done.[14]

The reporter from the local *Essex County Chronicle* was equally sceptical.[15] He turned up on the Maudes' doorstep at Wickham's Farm to be greeted by Mrs Maude, 'apparently a Russian lady', and was sent off into the fields where her husband was at work cutting kale.[16] It was his unorthodox dress which first caught the reporter's eye: he was wearing a tennis shirt and trousers with 'a kind of sombrero' on his head to keep off the sun. His feet were bare to the soil since, as he patiently explained, he had watched others and found that those who discarded their boots were less liable to catch colds. Here, clearly, was a reporter's delight, an eccentric, but the interviewer gave him plenty of room to explain the views of the colonists. He painted a picture of a colony where the communal will to live better was enough to bring about better living. You would look in vain for beef cattle on the estate because everyone had freely adopted vegetarianism. Alcohol would not be found here, even though there were no specific rules prohibiting it. In this world there was no need to assert by prescriptive rules the number of hours each individual should work in the common interest. 'Mr Maude', reported the interviewer, 'thought the example of work was infectious, and a man who was indolent would either be spurred to action by example or feel that it was no place for him'.

All, claimed Maude, disapproved of the competitive system and saw the motive power of commercialism as being avarice, whereas people ought to live with a desire to help others. "Our idea is to raise a sufficient food supply to keep us by cultivating the land. It is generally conceded, I believe, that the labourer, as a rule, receives 30 to 40 per cent of the value of his work in the shape of wages. We therefore think that we ought to get a decent subsistence by a cent per cent return". There was no reason, he believed, why this system should not be rolled out as a means of eventually relieving the slums of London.[17]

The colonists would, no doubt, have considered this a successful interview in expressing their vision and it must have contributed to the steady stream of inquisitive people who were now coming to Purleigh just to see these oddly clothed seekers after a better world. What they found could appear idyllic. In June a young Percy Redfern, an enquiring socialist who would one day become the historian of the co-operative movement, visited the Maudes and was taken down to meet the colonists:

> That evening, by a footpath through meadows, we all came to a house that Kenworthy and others had built with their own hands. Colonists and friends gathered here as one family, women in cotton frocks, men in working clothes, and a few children. There was conversation and music; women knitted or sewed; and Kenworthy read aloud from Brer Rabbit. Facing a window I could be aware of encircling, quiet fields, of distant woods, of a sea-like width of sunset. This was an island of kindness and peace.[18]

Chapter 6

The Settlement Unsettled

In one respect the smiling charmer that was Aylmer Maude was, in his newspaper interview in August 1898, successfully covering up some unfortunate cracks which were beginning to appear in the fabric of the colony. His account of the Thursday business meetings, where new candidates were 'admitted by election' and decisions were arrived at by consensus, was fair enough, but when he was asked how the colonists set about resolving any disagreements which might arise, his response was that no such question had yet arisen and in general, if unanimity on an issue did not appear the first time round, then the matter was brought back the next time and minority opposition would disappear. This was at best disingenuous, as we shall come to see.

Meanwhile, the life of the colony was being increasingly distracted by the issue of the Doukhobors which was coming to the boil more than 2,000 miles away. In February 1898, under pressure from St Petersburg, the Governor of the Caucasus announced that the Doukhobors would be allowed to leave Russia on condition that they raised the funding for their own exile and undertook never to return. News reached Britain in March and both Tchertkoff and Maude now swung into action, working to raise money specifically to fund the emigration and to seek a suitable home for those who left. In this they worked separately but alongside a committee of the Society of Friends who took an equal interest in a group in whom they saw many similarities of belief.

A number of possible sites for a new settlement were put forward. Tolstoy, who vigorously continued his support, suggested Texas, Turkestan, Manchuria and Cyprus. This last had come under English jurisdiction in 1878 and was, therefore, from the viewpoint of the Doukhobor sympathisers in Purleigh, the easiest to focus on. In May Arthur St. John wrote on their behalf to the Chief Secretary of the Cyprus government asking that consideration be given to a settlement there of, initially, some hundreds but eventually over 3,000 Doukhobor emigrants from the Caucasus.[1] He then swiftly left to pursue the cause in person in Cyprus. The response to his approach was supportive, though the condition was made that there should be guaranteed funding to move the immigrants on if the experiment failed. In June, the Prime Minister, Lord Salisbury, approved the scheme.

Early in July a small advance party of Russians arrived in Purleigh as a stopover on their way to Cyprus - no doubt adding to the bewilderment of the villagers.[2] There were two Doukhobor families, those of Peter Makhortov and Ivan Ivin, accompanied by Prince Dmitri Aleksandrovich Khilkov who, years before, in a Tolstoy-like moment of revelation, had divided up his estates among his peasants and attempted to live as one of them before himself being exiled to the Caucasus and taking up the cause of the sect. It was he who had urged Tolstoy to publicise their plight. At Tchertkoff's invitation they were joined by two other Russian émigrés. One was Pavel Biriukoff, whose account of the plight of the Doukhobors had formed the basis for Kenworthy's letter to *The Times* back in 1895. Exiled, like Tchertkoff, for his efforts in support of the Doukhobors, he was now working on their behalf with the Quakers. The other was a man of some notoriety. Peter Kropotkin, an important Russian scientist and geographer, born of a noble line, had abandoned both title and career for a life devoted to pursuing the goal, first of revolutionary change in Russia and then of anarchism. By the mid-1880s he had been imprisoned for his subversive activities in both Russia and France and was on the radar of the secret police across Europe. On being released in France in 1886 he had settled in England, still proselytising for the cause, writing, lecturing and co-founding the anarchist magazine, *Freedom*, to which Kenworthy was an occasional contributor. In 1896 he had moved to a small terraced house in Bromley, South London, and in that same year he had been invited, probably by Kenworthy, to speak in Croydon, eight miles away from his new home. Kropotkin was well known both to the Special Branch and to Okhrana, the Russian counter-terrorism agency, which ran agents in Britain, including one Vladimir Krivosh who had already visited Tchertkoff in Croydon. It is by no means fanciful to assume that either or

Peter Alexeievich Kropotkin, scientist and anarchist

both secret services would have been watching events at Purleigh carefully at this time, though the destruction of the vast majority of Special Branch records from this period makes it impossible to prove.[3]

The group were in Purleigh for perhaps a week, long enough to be welcomed by the colonists, eating with them in the large marquee which, now that numbers had grown, was serving as an open-air kitchen and dining space. But on 11 July Khilkov's group left to fulfil their task of scouting out possibilities in Cyprus.

They were back much more quickly than anyone had hoped or expected and they returned with stories of impoverished, sandy soil and a climate so different from that of the Caucasus that settlement would be impossible. Unfortunately word of the initiative had by now spread among the Doukhobors in the Caucasus. Anxious to leave before the mood of the local authorities changed, people began to sell up and move south to the port of Batoum on the Black Sea (the present-day Batumi), from where they hoped to take ship for Cyprus. By August, some 1,100 had reached the town, many of them sleeping in a disused factory as they awaited the next stage. In Britain the Quakers had spearheaded a campaign to raise the guarantees required by the government and a compromise settlement had been arrived at, amounting to £15 a head for each of those moving to Cyprus. To those unaware of the doubts already expressed in England the way seemed clear and the tide unstoppable. On 18 August a chartered French freighter left Batoum with 1,126 Doukhobors on board. When they arrived at Larnaca, Arthur St. John was there to meet them.

For a moment, Tchertkoff and Maude and their fellow colonists in Purleigh must have felt relief and pleasure that their efforts had paid off. But the story was far from over. It soon became clear that the Doukhobors were less than happy in their new setting. As Khilkov's party had warned, they had not been prepared for the unfamiliar heat, a far cry from their homeland, and the soil, parched and sandy, would take a long time to get used to. An early crop to help get them on their feet would be difficult to achieve. Lacking any established organisation, things rapidly became chaotic. Then dysentery and malaria struck and within a few months more than a hundred had died. To make matters worse, word was seeping through that no more of their brethren would be arriving; attention had shifted to another, very different, destination.

Back at Purleigh, news came early from St. John and from their Russian summer visitors that all was not well on Cyprus. It was clear that the remaining Doukhobors who wished to travel (well over 5,000 at the time) could not be allowed – and would have no wish – to follow. Alternatives needed to be considered.

Ironically, the answer had been found back in Purleigh before the exploratory party had left. In September 1897 Kropotkin, still an active and respected scientist, had travelled to Toronto to deliver some papers to a meeting of the British Society for the Advancement of Science. He then travelled across the country on the Canadian Pacific Railroad to British Columbia, returning slowly to get a feel for the country and its communities.[4] Among them he found several groups of Russian émigrés, transplanted to a largely undeveloped country where land was easily had and where the unorthodox stood every chance of being tolerated. In March 1898, having returned to England, he published, in the journal *The Nineteenth Century*, an account of his meeting with Mennonite farmers, another religious group, a considerable number of whom had fled Russia in the 1870s to avoid military service and who were now prospering in this new environment. Somehow this article had reached Tchertkoff's attention and it must have been in relation to this that he had invited Kropotkin to come to Purleigh for further discussion. Clearly the idea of Canada as an alternative destination had formed part of those discussions for Kropotkin had written from Purleigh on 10 July, seeking advice and assistance from a friend and acquaintance, James Mavor, the Scots-born Professor of Political Economy at the University of Toronto, who had, before emigrating, been active in Socialist circles in Glasgow:

Would the Canadian Government accept some 12,000 of these men (like Mennonites) and allow them to settle also in a block and have their own inner institutions. What course would you advise to take in these matters write to Ottawa? Or see some functionaries in London? Tchertkoff who is with Biriukoff and Khilkoff, the soul of this settlement, will write to you himself. The chief think [*sic*] is, to find at once as much material aid (they still have £6,000 for their 12,000 people, of common capital) – their own means being small: and second thing is to find in the meantime the means of transporting from Russia and getting all this mass of people.[5]

Kropotkin's confidence in Mavor was well placed. He wrote almost immediately to Tolstoy asking him for his views on the appropriateness of the Canadian climate for the Doukhobors and of their suitability for life in that country: "Are the people addicted to any of the outbursts or religious ecstasy resulting in sexual and other excesses that are alleged of the Skoptsi and Klebtsi?" Tolstoy's response was reassuring on all points.

Wheels turned quickly and on the strength of optimistic noises coming back from Canada, plans were soon being made for another reconnaissance mission, this time across the Atlantic. On 27 August Tchertkoff wrote to Mavor from Purleigh reassuring him, at Tolstoy's request, on the points he had raised and informing him that on 1 September the now much travelled Ivin and Makhortov families would leave Liverpool on their way to Canada. This time the party would be accompanied by Maude.[6] The same letter conveyed the news that the colonists at Purleigh had determined to commit £1,100 towards the cost of this emigration, enough, they believed, to resettle a hundred Doukhobors and underpin them for two months.

A group of Doukhobors newly arrived in Canada, 1902

The departure of Maude with the two Doukhobor families and the generous donation of funds to their cause must have seemed, to some at least, like the welcome drawing of a line under an unforeseen chapter in the life of the colony. Certainly it had given the colonists an opportunity to demonstrate their fellow-feeling with others who, like themselves, were attempting to find a new life unconstrained by external forces. But at the same time, for those focused on building their own viable community, it had proved a significant distraction. £1,100 was a philanthropic gesture on a grand scale but equally it was a serious depletion to the colony's finances, amounting to almost half of the capital initially put into the venture. It also came at a time when issues were developing which they could ill afford to ignore.

Early in the summer of 1898 two men had arrived at the colony seeking admission. The original Brotherhood Church members were increasingly being joined by newcomers who brought with them a mixed bag of aspirations and agendas.

These two came from the Midlands and were named Jack Brent and Owen Trafford.[7] They were accepted as novices but by July were causing problems. At a colony meeting that month (just a few weeks before Maude extolled to the press the unanimity of communal decisions taken at Purleigh) they were told that they were not considered suitable to become fully-fledged colonists. What they had done is not recorded. A *Manchester Guardian* journalist who had been among others descending on Purleigh in August was alone in picking up and reporting the issue, but only in the most anodyne way, no doubt a reflection of the guarded terms in which he had been told of the incident:

> The business of the colony is arranged at a weekly meeting of the members, and nothing is undertaken unless unanimity prevails. Up till now everything has gone smoothly. Two members who found that they did not see eye to eye with the others have left, but there has been no friction and no compulsion.[8]

Nellie Shaw, who was present at the meeting, admitted later to having at the time suspected class prejudice as lying at the root of the decision virtually to expel them. One of the two was a carpenter, the other an engineer. Certainly it is true that the background of those colonists we know about was largely clerical or professional, but even she, in the light of later events, went on to admit to doubts as to whether she had been right to see the clash of classes as the real problem.[9]

It seems not unrealistic, and indeed more plausible, on the basis of other comments made about this time, to suppose that this was somehow related to the problem of ensuring that all colonists 'pulled their weight' in terms of effort and output. Shaw herself, elsewhere in her memoir, talking about the requirement that everyone in the colony should be 'a good, energetic worker', drew attention to this: "There were no rules as such, but there was a certain standard of work or output which one was expected to attain, or he was treated to severe looks and more or less 'sent to Coventry'".[10]

Rereading Maude's August press interview it is possible to see more than a hint (if a muffled one) of this as a current issue, a difference of view among colonists: "Some members were desirous of making it [the colony] an economic success, and of opening a door of escape to the slaves of commercialism. Others were in favour of allowing anyone to join them who wished to do so". Just three months before, Hammond had explained in *The New Order* that decisions at the weekly colony meetings were only taken if unanimity of view was reached.[11] What had happened here? We simply do not know. Either that convention was breached – with dire results – or someone, perhaps Kenworthy, had asserted his will and influence to override the normal pattern of decision-making.

In the event, the decision to expel the two men caused an open rift between those who saw equal and fair input of labour as being an essential principle on which the colony should develop and those who held the more puristic view that the road to a better life should be open to all regardless of background or abilities.

Among the latter was another entrant who had been at Purleigh barely two months. Samuel Veale Bracher was a Quaker journalist from Gloucestershire with idealistic views, who brought with him a recent inheritance of £1,000 which, like Eiloart before him, he was looking to apply to an appropriate cause. There is some evidence that he had come to Purleigh with a view to learning about colonies before starting one himself nearer home.[12] In the event, Purleigh appeared to have fulfilled his needs – until, that is, the contentious July meeting at which he seems to have taken exception to the treatment of Brent and Trafford and reconsidered his future involvement. Instead, his thoughts returned to the idea of establishing a new, fresh colony, closer to his home ground and untrammelled by compromised principles.

The voicing of this idea opened a Pandora's Box. Feelings of discontent, hidden beneath a placid surface, now had a rallying point and a group of dissidents soon emerged, ready to quit Purleigh for a new venture elsewhere. Behind them, according to Nellie Shaw, lay an otherwise shadowy figure whom she calls Miss Clara Lee but who, in reality, was Charlotte Elizabeth Dunn, known to all as 'Lottie'. On the surface her credentials as a 'progressive' were impeccable. The daughter of Methodist farmers in the Vale of York, her brother Jonathan had turned towards spiritualism and the occult through the Theosophical Society and the Hermetic Order of the Golden Dawn while Lottie had become engaged with issues of social improvement, first by way of membership of the Fabian Society and then, in a more focused way, through the Sanitary Institute, a body the goal of which was the improvement of public health issues, particularly among the poorer classes. It may have been through either of these that she met Havelock Ellis, a progressive writer who was, at the time, turning his thinking and his pen to issues of sexuality, publishing his first volume on the subject, *Sexual Inversion*, in 1897. The two became friends.

It appears that Lottie was for a while associated with Aylmer Maude's household at Wickham's Farm but then moved to a cottage near Purleigh.[13] Here, according to Nellie

Shaw, she provided a refuge for those who wanted to get away from the colony for a while and discuss its problems and future at a safe distance. Among them she names Bracher, his Gloucestershire friend Joseph Burtt and Arnold Eiloart. It was here, she recalls, that she heard the idea first mooted of a breakaway in search of a new, differently principled colony.[14]

Once this plan developed and became known, the disappointment, particularly for Kenworthy, must have been deep. Significantly, those who were bent on leaving Purleigh included a number of 'founder colonists' who had come to Purleigh through the Croydon Brotherhood. Two of the three initial 'pioneers', William Sinclair and Sudbury Protheroe, decided to move on. Another couple who left were William MacDonald and his partner May Pinnell. MacDonald had started the Brotherhood tailoring and shoemaking business in Croydon along with Arthur Drover. Lottie Dunn would form part of the new group, taking with her Bracher and Burtt. Within a year Dunn and Bracher had married.

Perhaps the most significant loss, in practical terms, was that of Arnold Eiloart whose inheritance had been important both in acquiring the colony site and extending it and who had taken on the crucial role of secretary to the colony. For Eiloart to leave Purleigh at this point, with so much invested in it, both financially and intellectually, says much about the level of discontent in the air in that summer of 1898.

Their new home was to be at Whiteway in Gloucestershire, a few miles from Stroud, on 41 acres of fairly poor, exposed land with a cottage. It was bought for £450, a substantial part of that coming from Bracher. By the early autumn a first group was in situ and making plans for the future. Others followed. Sinclair and Protheroe, who had invested so much physical labour in the Purleigh venture since its beginning, and Eiloart, who had sunk so much of his money into it, decided to follow when they had finished the jobs they were engaged on. In October, Sinclair and Eiloart walked the 150 or more miles to Whiteway, relying on charity for food and accommodation along the way, determined to stick to their strict principle of living without money.[15] In February of 1899, Jeannie Straughan, another Brotherhood Church member, left to join Protheroe at Whiteway, where they began a 'free union'. The next month, having wound down their Brotherhood dressmaking business in Croydon, Nellie Shaw and her assistant Lucy Andrews joined the new community. Owen Trafford, one of the two men whose cause had led to the breakaway, had, on leaving Purleigh, gone for a while to join the Leeds community.[16] He too eventually moved to Whiteway where he met up again with Brent.

The loss to the Purleigh colony – and to the Croydon Brotherhood – was of a group of people who embodied a substantial share of that initial Tolstoyan idealism which had led them to Essex in the first place. For them the experiment was not over; it had simply entered a new chapter in a new setting. But there was a further, practical loss to the colony. Both Eiloart and Bracher had brought with them money or the promise of money. Eiloart had contributed hundreds of pounds from his first involvement, assisting both the initial purchase and subsequent growth of the estate. He had ensured the crucial involvement of William Hone through his contribution of a pound of week to the Hone family's upkeep. He was in the process of donating £1,200 to the Doukhobor cause. Bracher had made no such contribution but was looking for a worthy home for his legacy of a thousand pounds. This would now be put to the purchase of the Whiteway land. Moreover the Purleigh finances, already seriously depleted by the donation towards the Doukhobors, now took a further hit: it was generously decided that the 'leavers' should be reimbursed at least a part of any funds they had put into the colony's coffers.

Those who remained at Purleigh, however privately unsettled by the events of the summer, adopted a brave and positive face to the outside world, and in particular to others pursuing the better life. Herbert Archer, deputed to write in *The New Order* on the Whiteway defection, admitted that this had provided a 'temporary constraint' on the life of Purleigh, but turned quickly to the positive:

> In spite of the slight tension that has been felt we believe that all concerned in the formation of the new group are actuated by high motives and are sincerely desirous of furthering the same ultimate end that we ourselves are striving for. The colony has always hoped to be able to render assistance in the formation of new groups as occasion required and this development, though earlier than was anticipated, is, in a sense, a realisation of this hope.[17]

Nowadays we would call this 'spin'.

Despite these assurances it is reasonable to see this moment as a kind of tipping point in the fortunes of the Purleigh colony. The summer of 1898 had, to put it mildly, been a difficult one with the unexpected arrival of a score or more refugees, exotic in dress and speech, needing to be hosted and fed; the comings and goings of various figures bent on resolving problems far beyond the horizons of the labouring colonists; and the clear evidence, provided by the Brent–Trafford affair, that, despite the colonists' common pursuit of the dream of a shared and better life, views as to which path would or should lead them there were far from unanimous.

Chapter 7

Setting aside these considerable disruptions, the colonists' progress could still be justifiably seen as remarkable. It was, after all, less than two years since the pioneers had sunk their first spades into the unpromising Purleigh soil. The leading figures in the venture, those with access to wider audiences, seem to have gone out of their way at this time to make reassuring noises. It was in this summer that *The Clarion* and the *Essex County Chronicle* came to the village and were rewarded with Maude's positive account of communal activity and unanimous decision-making in the colony. An unidentified correspondent, writing in the *Labour Annual* for 1898, credited the colony with "a very promising beginning with real grit among the workers". In July, Kenworthy wrote in *St. George*, the newly established journal of the Ruskin Society of Birmingham, that, just a year before, the colony "was not much changed from the surrounding half-desolate fields of the country, where agricultural ruin has gone so far; but now you could not well miss it, because of four acres of market garden, a hundred feet of greenhouse, some finished new buildings, including a new brick house, and buildings going up".[1]

These additional buildings included a barn with a tiled roof for storage and a further single-storey house, this time for Kenworthy himself, who had previously been dividing his time between Croydon and rented accommodation at Woodham Ferrers, three miles away.[2] It was completed in November, with help from several men who had come south at Kenworthy's behest, having formed a co-operative carpentry and building enterprise in Morley outside Leeds, a spin-off from the Brotherhood Church there, on the development of which Kenworthy was now spending a great deal of time.[3]

He called the new house the Grey House and it would seem that he envisaged this as the future base for his activities. In the October issue of The New Order he had solicited views on his idea to establish a printing press at Purleigh, capable of printing *The New Order* and other future publications of the Brotherhood Publishing Company. There had, he indicated, been difficulties at Croydon, though they were not specified. In the event it is difficult to say how much time he spent at the Grey House. Apart from regular spells in Leeds, he was still active on many national stages, centrally involved in the establishment of the London Tolstoyan Society in 1898, a body which, once founded, he seems to have nurtured through its early life by presiding at most of the sessions. In 1899 he would be a speaker at, among other gatherings, the National Vegetarian Congress in London and he would continue his writings on Tolstoyan and related matters. It is little wonder that he had, in February 1898, handed over the editorship of *The New Order* to Frank Henderson, one of the early pioneers of the Croydon Brotherhood Church.

We have no record of how the absence of the 'big hitters', Kenworthy and Maude (who was in Canada), and of the colony secretary, Eiloart, who was now at Whiteway - left the governance of the colony. The 'Purleigh Notes' in *The New Order* continued to record progress despite a twelve-week drought across the autumn. By mid-October they were selling sacks of potatoes and tomatoes to 'friends' in London and looking to complete work on a new greenhouse and stable. Henderson, as editor of *The New Order*, while acknowledging in January 1899 that he had had nothing by way of notes from them for two months, reported them as being 'jolly enough round the festive board on Boxing Day'.

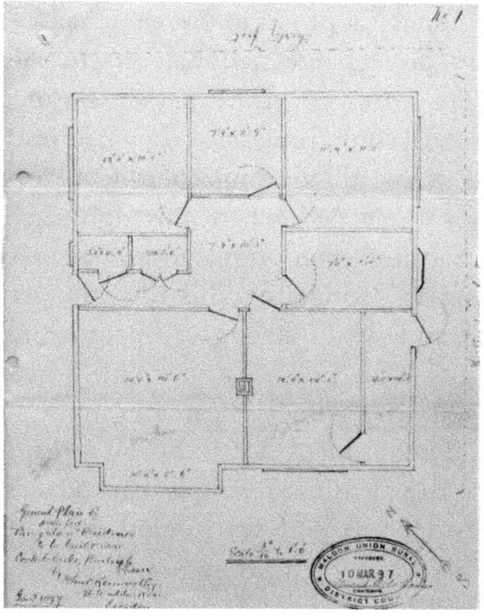

Plans for Kenworthy 's house in Purleigh as submitted to the Maldon Urban District Council in 1897

In some ways the colonists may have needed a quiet time to regroup after the dramas of 1898. If so, the respite was short. Tchertkoff had been left behind in his Mill Lane house, from where he kept up his contacts with Tolstoy, helping co-ordinate support for the Doukhobors and, wherever possible, raising awareness in England of Tolstoy and his beliefs. There is, however, no evidence that he ever played a leading role in the practical affairs of the colony.

By the early weeks of 1899 Maude and Kenworthy had returned, their vigour undiminished. In February, together with Tchertkoff and Johannes Van der Veer, the leader of the Tolstoyan movement in the Netherlands, they had gone to a public meeting in a local school, called by the Purleigh Parish Council to discuss a proposal by the Tsar of Russia for a conference to discuss international disarmament. Today this may seem far removed from parish business but parish councils were still something new; they had only been created in 1894 and were still finding their feet, uncertain of the boundaries of their power. In Purleigh the Council was headed by a battling, even pugnacious chairman by the name of John Freeman Boreham who ran the grocer's shop in Cock Clarks and was a strong campaigner for agricultural workers' rights. The previous year, having found a local footpath barred by a padlocked gate put up by a newly arrived farmer, he had taken matters into his own hands on behalf of the people of the parish and simply hacked off the lock. The matter came to court and was settled in Boreham's favour. Now his mind was set on getting an adequate water supply for the village.[4] In an election flyer he made it all too clear that his sympathies lay with the downtrodden of the village and not with the landowners and farmers:

> Persons who have some proverbial axe to grind, whose policy of land grabbing and wage lowering, depopulates whole villages, drives young men into the army and aged labourers into despair are not fit persons to represent you on Parish and District Councils, and it is for you to set your faces like a flint against these modern man-eaters.[5]

Given these anti-establishment views, the choice of debate may seem less surprising. Certainly it was one which was close to the hearts of the pacifist Tolstoyans and one wonders whether they had somehow been behind the staging of the meeting. In the event, a resolution that 'This meeting is of opinion that the slaughter of human beings is always wrong, whether desired by Governments or not' was easily carried, despite the fact that this was in the unsettled period between the first and second Boer Wars, when the sound of rattling sabres was never far away.

Spurred on by their success other resolutions were put forward, including one 'That this meeting expresses its sympathy with the seven thousand Doukhobortzi, who are now escaping from persecution in Russia, for refusal of military service'. Nor was this the last meeting the colony group chose to attend. The following month they returned, nagging away at questions about the fairness of the local rating assessment to smaller tenants and the provision (or lack of it) of allotments for labourers. It was difficult to tell who was egging whom on: the colonists or the councillors. The colonists were, it seems, far from isolating themselves in their idealistic plot, now openly taking their philosophical – even political – stances out into the community at large.[6]

Proselytising apart, the all-important matter of working the land which had, from the beginning, provided the practical as opposed to the philosophical fuel for the colony, continued, albeit at an inevitably reduced rate. The land did not let up in its demands. In a rainy January, forty tons of manure had to be shipped in by railway and carted along muddy, deep-rutted lanes to the colony, along with coal for the greenhouse boilers and cottage fires, bought in solidarity from a newly established collective of miners at Swadlincote in Derbyshire.[7] We learn that during the first half of 1899 corn, potatoes and a range of vegetables were grown, fruit trees were maintained and, in the two greenhouses, tomatoes were sown and grape vines planted. Continuing to look forward, work was started on a cartshed and money was donated to allow a second cottage to be built. In the absence of so much experienced labour, now being deployed at Whiteway, the lion's share must, however, now have fallen on the shoulders of the ever-faithful William Hone and a handful of others.

In his 'Purleigh Notes' in the May issue of *The New Order* Hone's tone was uncharacteristically weary, apologetic almost – even sad. The previous edition had carried an anonymous letter questioning the long term goals of the colony beyond that of sustaining the existing colonists: "May we come and share it with you by and by? Are you laying the foundation of a new life for us dirty, beer-swilling, helpless weaklings who have inch by inch sunk lower and lower in the slough of despond?" He could only reply, honestly and apologetically:

We are a small group in the midst of a worldwide movement towards a better and truer life for humanity. We are endeavouring by as honest labour as we are capable of to produce or exchange sufficient to supply our own needs of life and as much more as we are capable of, to help others. There are some things that have somewhat hindered this, and perhaps more things still have helped us: we have much to encourage us. It may not be the highest or best possible thing in life to aim at. We think it is a step worth taking, though our ideal is beyond it all. Not beyond the necessary productive labour, but beyond some present aspects of it.

As it happens, this would prove to be the last of the series of 'Purleigh Notes' to appear in *The New Order*. There was a bitter irony in the fact that Kenworthy's hopes of establishing a press at Purleigh had finally become a reality and this was the first edition to be produced there, though, as the editor admitted, some difficulties had arisen and he had been forced to reduce the number of pages.

By now the somewhat dejected Hone was among a rapidly dwindling band. Colonists were still slowly drifting away, some to follow on the first wave to Whiteway, others perhaps simply sensing the end and moving on to other ventures. In July 1899 a young Czech arrived at Purleigh. He came there by a tortuous route. Frantisek Sedlak, at 26, had already done much questing. He had tried the academic life and turned his back on it, joined the French Foreign Legion and deserted, been conscripted into the Austrian army and, on refusing to bear arms, had spent time forcibly confined in a lunatic asylum. In search of enlightenment he had walked all the way to Yasnaya Polyana and then been recommended by Tolstoy to travel to England,

Frantisek Sedlak

to sample the life of a colony. He went first to Newcastle, to the Clousden Hill colony, then walked the length of the country to Purleigh. His obvious resilience must have been momentarily challenged when, on finally arriving after yet another epic journey, he discovered that the colony was empty of all but the Hone family. Mercifully, there was an eventual happy ending to this erratic journey; Sedlak found his way to Whiteway and into a long-term relationship with Nellie Shaw. But the absence of anyone but the Hones at Purleigh suggests that the death knell had by then been sounded.

When the census enumerator came around in March 1901 he recorded what amounted to the vestiges of the colony. Kenworthy was not to be found at the Grey House; only Eleanor, his wife, and their daughter Emily were in residence.[8] Next door, in what was by then called 'Colony House', were the Hones, William and Lois, with their three sons, John, Albert and Arthur, together with Hubert Hammond. Next to them were Peter Harkin, the bricklayer, and his wife, but the next and last building on the colony plot was empty, the occupiers described as being 'away'.[9] Wickham's Farm, where the Maudes had lived, had changed hands and Tchertkoff and his entourage had gone from Mill House. Left behind, the last relict of the short-lived Purleigh Russian community was William Zhook, with his wife Dora, living in Hill Farm, just across the road from Mill House. It is ironic that Zhook, a radical journalist writing about Russian literature and new publications, became one of a small but growing band of writers who came to be critical of Tolstoy and in particular his pacifism at a time when the call for violent revolution in Russia was increasing.[10]

For Kenworthy the demise of the colony was a bitter reality to accept. It had been the centrepiece of his hopes for driving forward the work of the Brotherhood Church. He had made sure, through the pages of *The New Order*, that its progress was watched by fellow-thinkers across Britain and beyond. He could draw some comfort from the fact that regular reports were now appearing from emerging groups in Leeds, Blackburn and Whiteway but the quiet collapse of Purleigh, leaving greenhouses, livestock and fields untended, must have been both saddening and humiliating.

Amazingly, almost as though he were in denial, he chose this moment to publish in the columns of the October 1899 edition of *The New Order* what he called the Constitution of the colony (set out in full as Appendix I). Given the rebuttal of all forms of doctrinaire, coercive regulation and the emphasis on individual conscience which lay at the heart of the Church and of the colony at its foundation this was an extraordinary document. It began by setting out that the colony land should be vested in one or more trustees who were to be directed in their actions by a unanimous vote of the colonists, who should also elect a secretary and treasurer and any other officers deemed necessary to act on their behalf. It set out the arrangements for the admission of a candidate to the colony, requiring a unanimous vote by the colonists and making provision for postal voting on the part of any not in attendance at the appropriate meeting. It required applicants to subscribe to the constitution.

The rest of the document was largely taken up with the terms on which colonists might leave the colony. Such would-be leavers could make a declaration claiming back any property or moneys they had contributed and, if agreement could not be reached, making provision for an appropriate parcel of land to be leased to them for the term of their life, on condition that it was not sublet and that, if it were not properly cultivated, it would revert to the colony.

Perhaps Kenworthy hoped to staunch the flow of life-blood from the colony at Purleigh with this last-ditch attempt at regularising things. Perhaps he hoped to attract new colonists on these terms. If he did, it did not work and in publishing the document he was, in reality, making a dramatic admission of defeat. Not only did its terms concede the impossibility of unconditional common ownership (at least where Purleigh was concerned) but its very form, with its rigid and carefully worded legality, was exactly what Tolstoyan anarchism abhorred.

Even before the constitution was published, Aylmer Maude had taken the step of writing to Tolstoy to tell him the colony was dying. By the time the Master replied, on 15 December, with somewhat disparaging comments on the misguidedness of colonies, there was no doubt. It was dead.

Tolstoy, the master in whose name this venture had been undertaken, had from the beginning been inconsistent on the subject of colonies. He had often encouraged those who embarked on such experiments and had even directed the occasional follower, like Sedlak, towards them, but he nevertheless clung to his preference for men and women to concentrate on refining the purity of their own hearts. When colonies failed he was always able to point to their unpreparedness of heart as the cause of failure. So it was in his reply to Maude:

> The failure of life in the Colony, about which you wrote, is only an indication that the form of life which was chosen for the Colonists for the realisation of their spiritual needs was not adequate. When a definite inner content exists in man, it finds for itself a corresponding form - generally un-consciously, i.e. when one is not thinking about the form, and when the form is not defined in words.[11]

He was more overt in a letter written to *The New Order* after the Purleigh collapse, a letter which began "What matters it that communes have broken up?"

> The standing on the pillar, the retiring into the desert, and the living in a commune may be temporarily necessary for some people, but as a permanent form, it is evident sin and folly. To live a

pure and holy life on the pillar, or in the commune, is impossible because man is deprived of one half of life – of intercourse with the world, without which his life has no meaning.[12]

It was not in Tolstoy's character to say "I told you so", but he could perhaps fairly have pointed to views he had expressed to Kenworthy three years before when the idea of a colony was beginning to develop in the Brotherhood Church.

> Were one's friends to direct toward their inner spiritual growth all the portion of attention and energy which they devote to the sustainment of the outer form of a community amongst themselves, it would be better both for them and God's cause. Communities and external organisations seem to me to be lawful and useful only when they are inevitable consequences of a corresponding inner state.[13]

Chapter 8

Post Mortems

Leaving aside Tolstoy's own diagnosis, it is impossible to identify a single, overriding cause of the collapse of the Purleigh colony. Certainly the trigger was pulled with the departure for Whiteway of the breakaway group in the summer of 1898. With them went much of the spirit which had brought it into being in the first place.

But the reasons for that split have been blurred by the passage of time and the lack of contemporary accounts. There were those who, later on, chose to look back to the events of those few short years and, with the benefit of hindsight, pronounce their individual verdicts. All were coloured by their experiences in later life.

Nellie Shaw was one such. When, in 1935, she wrote her account of the Whiteway colony, of which she was one of the founder-members, she could look back across nearly four decades of living in and as part of that colony.[1] Though by then it was undoubtedly different in its governance and pattern of daily life from the early aspirations of those who walked and cycled across the country to found it, it was at least still there. Her verdict on Purleigh and its demise was crushing:

> We cannot help contrasting the two colonies – Purleigh and Whiteway – the former, although it started very simply, yet soon receiving help, and being almost petted by moneyed people (these, in the long run, not proving a real help, but rather the reverse, for the spirit which proved the downfall of Purleigh was largely generated by those who were not workers, but honorary colonists: money again tilting the scale and giving a preponderance of

influence to those who, as mere men, might not have counted so much) while, in the latter case, we at Whiteway were up against hard circumstances from the very first.[2]

It was, then, in her eyes, what we might call the outer ring of Purleigh – Kenworthy in and out of the Grey House, Maude in Wickham's Farm and Tchertkoff in Mill House – each with his own côterie and sphere of influence – that weakened the spirit and moral fibre of the colony itself. Certainly each of them was a powerful character: Kenworthy passionate, even intolerant, in his Tolstoyan mission, Maude affable but quietly determined and Tchertkoff charismatic but highly flammable; "The intensity of Mr Tchertkoff is almost over-powering", as one newspaperman described him at a first meeting.

As for Shaw, so too did the experience of the Purleigh years turn sour for Aylmer Maude. When, in 1904, he published his account of the Doukhobors, *A Peculiar People*, he described Eiloart as "an eccentric member of a queer Colony that had a brief existence in Purleigh in Essex", the only mention of the colony in the whole book. Clearly the bare-footed, sombrero-wearing, kale-cutting enthusiast whom the *Essex County Chronicle* reporter had, just six years before, described as 'a distinguished member of the Brotherhood', had become disenchanted.[3] When he completed the first volume of his life of Tolstoy in 1908, his Purleigh years were reduced to a single sentence in the Preface: "Some ten years ago we took part in an unsuccessful 'Tolstoy' Colony". But, in subsequently writing the second part he was more reflective. Some of the colonists, he argued, were disappointed to find that the rejection of conventional ways of carrying on industry and business did not automatically lead to 'efficient or harmonious activity', while those who were most committed to Tolstoyan teachings tried to keep faith with them but, in so doing, looked elsewhere for the causes of failure. "The more zealous partisans of the movement, reluctant to admit that there was a flaw somewhere in the teaching, preferred to lay the blame on one another". He was explicit in his own blame-placing: "Quarrels were therefore frequent and Kenworthy's eccentricities, which later on developed into insanity, helped to involve and embitter these disputes".[4] Kenworthy's later instability is a matter of record but Maude's harsh verdict on the man was no doubt encouraged by the fact that he, Kenworthy, had served a writ for libel on him in 1903 following a dispute over the Brotherhood Publishing Company's exclusive right to publish Tolstoy's works in England.

It was quarrelling then that ultimately was, in Maude's eyes, the downfall of the community. "Those of us who kept our sanity, did not always keep our tempers", he admits. But beyond this, his allocation of blame is cloaked in vagueness and ambiguity. Both Tchertkoff and Kenworthy are lashed by his tongue but when it comes to the nub it is not clear at whom he is pointing the finger. "The cause of the failure of our movement lay in the confusion which resulted from trying to combine a teaching of poverty, self-abnegation and brotherhood, with the autocratic administration of large affairs, and the irresponsible power of one man". Is that man Tchertkoff, whom he is about to accuse of maladministration and misappropriation of funds during the Doukhobor resettlement in Canada; or Kenworthy, whom he has just accused of eccentricity verging on insanity?

Certainly there is an inherent contradiction between the open-armed approach of welcoming all to the colony, regardless of ability, resources or aspiration and the decision -

by whomsoever it was made – to bar Brent and Trafford. Just months before, Hubert Hammond had written in *The New Order*:

> We have no rules, each one is left to do as he or she likes, held in check only by their own good sense, and the general opinion of his comrades. Neither have we any fixed rules about the admission of new members. Some have brought money with them, others have not. Usually we try to give people wishing to join a clear statement of our position, and leave it to them to decide whether they will cast in their lot with us to work towards the ideal or not.[5]

Three months later came the expulsion.

Roads seem to lead us back to the personality of Kenworthy and his mental state. Over the years, his commitment to the letter of Tolstoy's thinking and teaching (as he interpreted them) seems to have grown more and more intransigent. No definitive evidence has so far come to light that it was Kenworthy's insistence that new entrants to the colony had unimpeachable Tolstoyan credentials which led to the dismissal of Brent and Trafford and the Whiteway breakaway, but we do know that when the young Percy Redfern had visited Purleigh with a view to joining, he had been subjected to an intensive barrage of questioning by Kenworthy:

> Did I not admit the falsity of existing economic and social relations? Could any man live by falsehood? Was not truth life, and life truth? Could I not trust to truth for my living? Would God, being absolute truth, let any man serve truth and starve?[6]

Not surprisingly Redfern, despite an idyllic evening shared with the colonists, did not choose to pursue a future at Purleigh and in his recollection of that meeting he put his finger upon perhaps the key issue: "Actually, the founder of the colony represented, in this inquisition, the spirit that already was disintegrating his own creation".

Salome Hocking, in her novelistic account of the colony, put her finger on a fundamental source of tension when she recounted a conversation with another colonist about 'Fred Firman' (her personification of Kenworthy) known around the colony as 'The Boss':

> "Fred Firman was the man who transacted the business [of the purchase of the land] but the money to buy the land was found by four of the original colonists. Fred Firman isn't the boss any more than any other member. That is one of Billy's [another colonist's] labels, and as usual it sticks, for Fred is a bit inclined to lay down the law when he comes".

> "… He looks like a man who would find a difficulty in keeping his temper under control if he were thwarted. And yet on certain sides of his nature I should say he is easily influenced".

> "Yes, you are quite right, he is easily influenced, especially by idealistic people".

That ambiguity about role, in the minds of both Kenworthy and the colonists, proved disastrous.[7]

Kenworthy himself had, not surprisingly, a different view of the reasons for the colony's collapse. By February 1900, when he came to give his own verdict on the failure of Purleigh, he had satisfied himself of the roots of the problem: 'lusts' and 'schemes' were to blame. 'Lusts' were the 'passions, appetites and desires of the body', the failings of 'people largely of animal nature': "Eating and drinking, seeing and hearing, clothing and housing themselves, and especially gratifying themselves sexually with companionships or in marriage". 'Schemes' were private agendas, deceptively hidden from others, the common currency of the corrupt modern world. They had infected the colony:

> Too readily seeing each others' faults and errors, while slow to realise our own, fearing, in consequence, that others would go wrong, we began to frame each his own separate scheme for the common good. ... Disappointment, ill-feeling, recrimination grew up, and what lust began, scheming finished.[8]

Writing a year later in 1901, in what was to become his *Tolstoy, His Life and Works*, he seemed to have climbed free of the wreckage and distanced himself from blame, a casualty not a cause:

> Our efforts in England, always keenly watched by Tolstoy, about four years ago resulted in the formation of a 'Colony' at Purleigh, in Essex, where I, with others, came to reside. It is no part of the purpose here to describe the history and fate of the venture. Two years ago, it began a process of disintegration. My place was simply to exhaust my resources, and begin afresh when the end came. Not want of means, not want of recruits, but want of character, brought the crash. And not merely from Tolstoy's warnings, but from prior experience, I knew what to expect, and was prepared, as well as one can be, for a certain kind of ruin.[9]

In other words the colonists, or at least some of them, had not lived up to expectations, neither his nor Tolstoy's. There is something in that sentence which seems to bear out Redfern's recollection of his questioning by Kenworthy and to chime with Maude's talk of 'more zealous partisans of the movement'.

Kenworthy's focus on 'lusts' opens up a window onto another aspect of doctrinaire intolerance which is little mentioned by the players in the Purleigh drama but which almost certainly played a part in the decision of the Whiteway group to leave. Our sometimes monochrome image of late Victorian preoccupations may have diminished the importance, in progressive circles of the time, of what was sometimes referred to as the 'S.Q.'. Nellie Shaw provides a clue:

> As time went on, it became apparent, to some at any rate, that there were two essentials for a colonist: one was that he must be a good, energetic worker, and the other that he must hold the orthodox Tolstoyan views regarding sex.[10]

Tolstoy's wild inconsistencies in this area are well known: that after a promiscuous youth he had married and fathered thirteen children but that, as his ideas developed, he increasingly preached that the only proper route to salvation was a life of chastity or at least a life dedicated to pursuing the goal of chastity. Shaw reveals that, both in the weekly meetings in the colony and in private conversations, this was a regular theme:

> Protracted but interesting discussions used to take place, many if not most revolving around what was popularly known as the 'S.Q.', i.e. the sex question. Some who were true followers of Tolstoy on the

question of bread-labour were not able to accept in its entirety his very drastic teaching on the other matter and to be looked on with approval this seemed to be necessary. So, in this way, a kind of orthodoxy with respect to work and views on sex began to arrive – which had a direct bearing upon subsequent events that led to the formation of Whiteway Colony.[11]

Kenworthy's own views took Tolstoy's teaching to an almost virulent extreme of puritanism. He had set them out in a two-part article on Marriage in the *The New Order*:

> Can any line of 'rational' conduct be found for men and women in the sex-relations which will not cost them moral struggle and physical self-denial to maintain? The answer must be: None whatever. In the sex-relation, humanity is face to face with a force, a passion, which must be fought and conquered. Every normal mature man and woman knows this is true. If that struggle be not undertaken, by each individual, animalism, degeneracy, death, destroy the life. Perfectly allowed by every human being, this ideal would mean the extinction of the present race of animal men, certainly. But is that a loss, weighed against the gain of perfected human souls?[12]

How far Kenworthy's view pertained among the colonists we cannot know but it seems significant that, while we have no record of any new liaisons or 'free unions' taking place at Purleigh, the early history of Whiteway is peppered with such relationships developing and being accepted as part of the fabric of the community's life. Bracher married Lottie Dunn in 1899. William Protheroe also committed to a free relationship, he with Jeannie Straughan. Eiloart entered into a free union in 1899 with May Pinnell, of the Croydon Brotherhood Church, she having dissolved a similar three-year old partnership with another Croydon progressive, William MacDonald. When Kenworthy had, in *The New Order*, somewhat summarily and coyly announced that 'marriage' back in July 1896, (thereby quietly betraying his position over the issue) they had felt obliged to correct the impression he had given that this was an orthodox wedding: "We have set ourselves in opposition to the ordinary conventions of the day, and consequently there was no religious or legal ceremony whatever".[13] Eiloart and Pinnell eventually entered into a conventional marriage, but not until 1927.

Authoritarianism, dogmatism, disagreements of principle, peer pressure, the undue influence of money, personality clashes, weakness of character or lust: perhaps, at the end of the day, all of them played a part in the colony's downfall.

Perhaps, also, there were just too many views of how the colony should develop. They came to this spot, these seekers after a better life, with what appeared to be a common goal, whether that was couched in Tolstoyan terms or in a more personal vision. They had to be strong-minded and determined to make the break with everyday life and come into the stripped-down intensity of the colony. But gradually, while working with their fellow-colonists and exchanging views on personal and communal development, it became apparent that there were as many different visions of 'the better life' and how to achieve it as there were colonists. Coming together was one thing; holding things together was another – and much more taxing – issue.

Chapter 9

Afterlife

The ripples from the Purleigh débâcle continued to spread for a while. Within the pages of *The New Order* there was a more searching examination of some of the issues exposed by recent events: of free love, of the significance of the attempt by some to live without money, of the basic aims and principles of the Brotherhood Church. It led one reader to complain that *The New Order* had become too high in its ambitions and demands for 'poor beggars like me'.[1] There was still good news to be found in the paper: news from Whiteway and from the Doukhobors, now settling in Canada, hopes for a new Brotherhood group in Huddersfield and a new Brotherhood colony at Blaricum in Holland. But something of the old spirit seemed to have gone; the differences seemed somehow greater than the sense of unity, just as they had in the last days of Purleigh.

Percy Redfern, who had visited Purleigh in 1898 and was now founder and Secretary of the Manchester Tolstoy Society, writing in the *Labour Annual* for 1900 of the problems and difficulties confronting colonies, pointed to the contradiction between the strength of individual character and personal belief that led men and women to join such ventures and the need to work together and subsume some at least of that individualism in order to produce a cohesive working community. Was he perhaps remembering his questioning at the hands of Kenworthy a year or more before?

It was all made worse by Kenworthy himself who, after six months of silence in the journal he had founded, reappeared to criticise its editor, Frank Henderson, who had taken over the role from him three years before. "Since that time, my own views and feelings have been less and less represented in the paper, and the unfortunate expressions in it, upon the use of money in the Christian life, and above all, upon the terrible perversion of Christian sex-morality which developed at the Whiteway Colony in Gloucestershire, have caused me the greatest anxiety and pain".[2] It evoked a powerful defence from Tom Ferris, a leading figure in the Leeds group, criticising Kenworthy for his authoritarian demand for a single view – his view – and defending the 'broad church' of views expressed in *The New Order*.[3]

The failure of the Purleigh experiment dealt what would turn out to be a death-blow to the Brotherhood Church in Croydon. The transfer of so much hope into the colony venture deprived the Brotherhood of some of its most lively and determined members and of much of the energy which they had taken with them. With its name gone, the church simply faded into the complex landscape of socialist activity in the town. In *The New Order* of July 1899, Nellie Shaw announced the closure of the Brotherhood Dressmakers. It had lasted four years and given employment to four people. It had never, she admitted, made a profit and they had found themselves, to their disappointment, making clothes for 'fairly well-off people'. This was not the future they saw for themselves and she and her partner Lucy Andrews were off to Whiteway. With that, the lights were put out and the door closed on the last of the Croydon Brotherhood Industries. Now that the very name Brotherhood Church had been dropped, its meeting place became, quite simply, Tamworth Hall. Its energies seem eventually to have found a new home in the Croydon Social Union, set up in 1904, its primary object described as 'the consideration and discussion of social and religious questions in the light of the best thought of the day with a view to the furtherance of the principle of Brotherhood in all the relations of life'. Tchertkoff, St. John and Maude all spoke at its meetings. Of Kenworthy there was no sign.[4]

The Brotherhood Church, Croydon, seen in 2017

For Purleigh, however, there was to be a curious and unexpected afterlife.

Back in Leeds, in a pattern which will be all too recognisable, divisions had begun to appear over the issue of whether members of the workshop should contribute regular hours of labour or should be free to play their part as their circumstances permitted. The predictable break-up ensued and a group of key members left in 1900 to join a second of Kenworthy's offspring groups, this time in Blackburn, newly formed in 1898 and known as the Christian Communist Friends. Here they established another electrical business. Details of their time there are few and far between but it seems clear that there lingered, at least among the more doctrinaire followers, the dream of a territory or piece of land in which their tenets could be lived out without interference.

There had been talk for some time in both Leeds and Blackburn of establishing a base in the country but nothing had come of it. Now the idea of reawakening a colony at Purleigh emerged. Some of the community already knew it; there had been a degree of traffic between the groups. The land remained in the hands of the Brotherhood Church and Kenworthy's home address was, at least nominally, still in Purleigh. That he was not involved in this rebirth seems improbable in the extreme, though he would later come to say that it had happened against his wishes and those of the Hone family.[5] Either way, in September 1901 the Brotherhood Church of Blackburn issued the news to the press of its intention "to emigrate from Blackburn to Purleigh, near Maldon, in Essex, where 20 acres of land had been offered them as a site for a colony".[6] Shortly thereafter a small group of émigrés from the north arrived. We know the names of six of them: Arthur Taylor and Bertie Rowe, Tom and Lilian Ferris and Ernest and Jenny Ames, who took with them their two children.[7]

They were an intense group. Tom Ferris, who had previously criticised Kenworthy in the pages of *The New Order* and had now become among its most prolific contributors, had once expounded his beliefs to a reporter on the *Blackburn Times*:

> The misery of this world is caused by fear. Nearly all evil and misery, reduced to the lowest terms, revolve themselves into fear of our fellow men. Obviously the secret of happiness is the absence of fear. Therefore we say that force in any form is opposed to love. Hence we regard a soldier as a

murderer, and a policeman as a thoroughly unchristian officer. We don't believe in defending our lives, or holding property by force.[8]

He went on to explain his abandonment of the use of money:

I don't believe in the use of money, and do not use it. Money represents a system of exchange which is responsible for many of the evils of life. It is an expression of fear that our needs not be supplied out of love.

Already he had clashed with the law over his refusal to take part in the 1901 census; it cost him a £1 fine. When he had chosen on Christmas Day in 1898 to enter into an informal marriage with fellow-colonist Lilian Hunt, arguing that a legal marriage was a form of compulsion, they had both been expelled from the Quaker church of which they were members.

He was not alone in the vehemence of his beliefs and the degree to which he was prepared to defend them. Another inflexible colonist was Arthur Taylor who, some years later, would challenge the Leeds Education Committee in court over their demand that his child should attend school, part of what he described as "a great system of false education to maintain the whole tyranny of sham, and to train the children in subservience to its authority, so that they may have no higher outlook than your foul laws permit, and may bow down to the prince of this world instead of the Son of Man".[9]

Though by now well versed in the vicissitudes and problems of communal life lived on the sharp edge of idealism, this small group were essentially townsfolk who had little or no experience of the rural life. On their arrival in Purleigh they took up residence together in the colony's now deserted barn. Hone, who was still living in his cottage with his wife and three sons, does not appear to have involved himself with them. He had, perhaps, had enough of colonies. It left the urbanites in the midst of a substantial and well equipped smallholding but with no skills or experience in managing the land or producing food from it. Ferris appealed to friends in *The New Order* in November to consider and assist with their immediate needs, set out - exhaustively - as food, axe, wheelbarrow, spades, picks, forks, hoes, rakes, water-carrier, pruning tools, fruit trees, nut bushes, plants, seeds, hand cornmill, lime, and information - about nut growing, fruit drying, bee-keeping, and the preparation of nuts and fruit for food.[10] Their lack of preparation and sheer ignorance is all too clear. With their determination to avoid the use of money (and with none in their pockets anyway), the prospects were grim. Their winter must have been miserable in the extreme; but things were about to get worse.

In 1901 smallpox and the fear of smallpox gripped the country. Major cities like Liverpool and Glasgow were badly affected. In London, cases reached a peak in March 1902, when over 1,600 people were being treated for the disease. In Essex more than 800 cases were recorded in the first quarter of the year. Across the country, every effort was made to halt its spread.

In February a doctor visited the school in Cock Clarks to vaccinate the children but the following month, at exactly the moment of the peak of the epidemic in London, the school log-book records that he returned to ensure the job was complete "because a tramp suffering from smallpox has been wandering about this neighbourhood. He is now removed to Small-Pox hospital at Totham".[11] In the event the children were unscathed but, down the road, the colonists were less lucky. They had all refused vaccination. Following their principle of giving refuge to anyone who came to the colony, they had taken the tramp in. Again the log-book tells the story:

> March 24th: Dr Thresh's Assistant called again today. Some of the Colonists helped the poor sick 'Tramp', not knowing that he was suffering from Small-pox. This evening a man from the Colony was taken to the Isolation Hospital suffering from Small-pox. They are afraid others are sickening. The Doctor says the 'Gradys' and 'Cottees' must not attend school for a fortnight because the Gradys have been backwards & forwards to the Colonists Barn where they live.

> April 21st: Seven of the colonists besides the one before mentioned have taken small-pox and are being nursed in their own barn in the village.

> May 2nd: A poor man at the Colony barn died this week of the Small pox.[12]

That the principle of open-handed hospitality should have had such a dire consequence was a bitter and ironic outcome and one not lost on the local press:

> One of their principles is that they shall never 'turn the stranger from the door' and in obedience to this command, they appear to have offered free and open hospitality to a tramp, regardless of his dirty condition and not knowing, probably, that he was suffering from small-pox. When the visitor was

officially declared to be infected with the dread disease – in spite of their professed belief in 'all men's good' – they refused to be re-vaccinated, and who can be surprised at the result.[13]

The experience might have finished off a less determined group but they had few options. Driven to Purleigh in search of a life on the land free of all external constraints and impositions, they were in reality a more ideologically coherent band than their predecessors on the site. On the other hand, without the help of someone like Hone they were hopelessly ill-prepared for a life of self-sufficiency, especially one which renounced the money economy and depended therefore upon barter or exchange of their own produce. Where else was there to go?

The smallpox incident had brought the group unwillingly to the attention of the local press. It would not be the last time. In the following year their anarchist beliefs brought them into collision with the law. In that year Jenny Ames had given birth to twins. In August 1903 a summons arrived from the Dengie Petty Sessions at Maldon; Ernest Ames was being charged with failing to register a birth as required by law. When the Registrar had delivered the summons to him he had refused to attend the court and said there was no point in fining him since he was penniless and, if he had to go to jail, so be it. He stuck to his guns and, instead, submitted a letter to the court explaining his actions:

In order to make our position quite clear, we refuse to register ourselves or our children as subjects of any coercive administration. We do this in the interests of humanity, for no salvation can be found for men save in repentance of the ways of the world, and in turning to Him who is the Way, the Truth and the Life.[14]

He was promptly fined 20 shillings with costs or 14 days in prison. Presumably he served the latter.

Apart from these occasional brushes with the press we have little more information on the later life of this second colony than the details recounted by A.G. Higgins in his *History of the Brotherhood Church*, compiled in the late 1970s.[15] This draws on recollections of members of the Brotherhood, both oral and written, but does not acknowledge these sources in detail. According to Higgins' account, the group continued to live in the barn after the smallpox episode but developed an interest in spiritualism (an interest they shared with Kenworthy). In the course of a séance, Tom Ferris was instructed by the visiting spirit of St. Porphyrius to go to Russia in an attempt to convert Tolstoy to spiritualism. In the winter of 1902/3 he and Bertie Rowe somehow, without the use of money, found their way across Europe and through a Russian winter to Yasnaya Polyana. The trip was less than successful. Tolstoy, increasingly tetchy in his old age, was dismissive of their mission and Bertie Rowe experienced some form of mental disorder in which he threatened to kill his travelling companion. How much weight to put on this account it is difficult to say but the characters involved seem all to have been capable of jousting with improbability and winning.

This time news of their penniless journey to Russia attracted the eye of the national press (though without mention of Rowe's instability). Ames leapt quickly to steer the story away from the imputation that the mission had been inspired by a spiritualist visitation – still viewed by a large part of the population (and the press in particular) as being tinged with weirdness, if not insanity. The true purpose of their journey, he claimed, was to persuade Tolstoy to recognise that, over and above his belief in the centrality of the Sermon on the Mount, he should recognise the power of what Ames called 'the miraculous teaching' of the Gospel. By placing one's faith firmly in Christ's ability to provide for human needs, men can avoid the daily compromises which frustrate their spiritual goals. "All things are possible if men unite their wills to God's, because without attaching to it that belief in the power of God – or Love – to overcome all material difficulties, men will inevitably compromise with their consciences, making their material needs the excuse". Ames was forced by the reporter to confess that, though his colleagues had so far had four interviews with Tolstoy, he had refused to budge. "What he says is that he has nothing further to learn in the direction of the power of spiritual law over the material universe".[16] One can almost hear the sound of a door slamming.

Ames took advantage of this press opening to paint a picture of a thriving community of 'about twenty adults and a dozen attached to the settlement', about half of whom, he explained, were out and about, nursing and preaching. The land was under cultivation and the produce which was not consumed by the colonists was given away or exchanged without the intervention of money.[17] It all sounds idyllic and it is difficult to accuse a man of such high principle of deception but nowhere else is this high number of colonists mentioned. In April 1902 Dr Thresh had reported seven men and three women in the colony barn, with three children. Ames was perhaps using the phrase 'attached to the settlement' in the loosest possible way.

This attempt at putting a positive spin on the behaviour of the colonists and their life in Purleigh was not helped by a second intervention, this time from an unexpected (and unwelcome) quarter. Kenworthy seized upon the opportunity to leap in, pointing out that the present colony (interestingly he makes no mention of the first, Croydon, group) had been founded by himself and seven others and setting out his own stripped back account of his purpose and vision: "a simple form of Christianity with which Quaker doctrine is identical; the furtherance of Trade Unionism and Co-operation as solutions of the problem of social reconstruction, and the cultivation of healthy arts and crafts".[18] Quickly and firmly he distanced himself from the Blackburn group because "they would not work, and professed an impossible doctrine about not using money". He then delivered the coup de grâce: since the other six 'founders' had gone away, the title to the land now reverted to himself and William Hone. He had given them notice to move on.

There was no shifting of the ground and no compromise. Ames had already recognised this in his interview with the *Daily News*. Kenworthy (identified by him only as 'a man who was formerly a supporter of the Brotherhood') knew, he asserted, that their conscience would not allow them to defend their right. They could only appeal to his better judgment. It did not work. The return of the pilgrims from Russia to Purleigh in June 1903 was followed rapidly by the end of their rural experiment. The remains of the group returned north, to more familiar terrain.

It is hard not to question Kenworthy's state of mind at this time. No sooner had he reclaimed the colony land than he sued the *Daily News* for damages of £10,000 for an alleged libel in an article about the issues at Purleigh. Specifically Kenworthy objected to the passage which read:

> In pursuance of the Christ life, the Brotherhood cannot recognise existing laws. For instance, a man who was formerly a supporter of the Brotherhood threatens to take their land from them, knowing that their conscience will not permit them to defend their right.

This he saw as a misrepresentation of his right as a landowner to reclaim his land. The case came to the King's Bench in November with Kenworthy representing himself and calling himself 'a solicitor'. The judge, Mr Justice Bigham, seems to have seen the case as an opportunity to poke fun at the wayward views of Kenworthy and the colonists, not least when he discovered that Kenworthy had applied to the *Daily News* for £30 to enable him to bring the case against them. The case was dismissed, having achieved nothing but a public humiliation for Kenworthy and his aspirations over nearly a decade.[19]

As for the northern colonists, they set up a business in Beeston, on the edge of Leeds, making sandals, boots and woollen clothing and interspersed this with the writing of pamphlets and clashes with the authorities on issues of conscience, including another summons to Ames, this time for the maintenance of his three children, issued by his wife Jenny, with whom he had entered into a form of marriage in 1899 in the Brotherhood Church but whom he had left, it was stated, in 1903 on marrying an 18-year old at Purleigh.[20] The coming of the 1st World War found a number of the members of the Brotherhood declaring themselves – and suffering – as conscientious objectors. Ferris and Sidney Overbury were arrested and locked up for publishing an anti-war leaflet, Frank and Alfred Higgins also spent time in prison. Eventually, in 1921, the group resumed their quest for land and settled in Stapleton, near Pontefract in Yorkshire. The colony they established is still there to this day.

Chapter 10

Legacies

When the last of the colonists closed the barn door behind them for the final time and set off to head north, the Purleigh chapter in the history of utopianism came to an end – almost. In April 1905, the *Essex Newsman* published a short article under the heading 'Life under the sky at Purleigh. City men who have abjured the shelter house'.

> Two men have been living an open-air life at Purleigh, near Maldon, for two years. One of them holds a responsible position in a large shipping office; the other, who has cut himself entirely adrift from City life, devotes himself to agricultural work. They are the owners of three acres of freehold land on which stands a tent, which is their guest chamber. It is furnished with a small table, roughly made from a tree which once grew on their estate, and a number of cooking utensils. Unless the rain drives them to the shelter of the tent they sleep in the open. Their beds, which are spread behind the tent, consist of macintosh ground sheets and woollen sleeping sacks and rugs. Both the men are vegetarians, and belong to a sect which discountenances the taking of animal life. They declare that they do not know the meaning of illness, and one of them, who was once the weakling of the family, has developed into a man of great physical strength.

These were not the same acres and this was in no sense a continuation of the Brotherhood colony. These were men for whom, probably, Tolstoy meant little or nothing, who would in no sense describe themselves as a colony, who were driven 'back to the land' by a simple desire for a healthy life.

They were not alone. Indeed, one might see them as the precursors of a much larger movement which would, in the inter-war years, see large areas of southern Essex given over to small plots of land (the 'Plotlands') taken over by working folk escaping, either full- or part-time, the drudgery and grime of London.[1]

The idea of a colony did not, however, die with the Purleigh venture. Indeed, in the time of its short life, the notion of colony-building had spread more widely. Essex land still remained relatively cheap and therefore attractive. The exploratory party which had come to Purleigh from Croydon in the summer of 1896 must have felt that they were bringing a new way of thinking and living to an otherwise depressed agricultural area, weighed down by aged and creaking systems of land tenure and taxation. This was also territory unknown to them. They may have been full of optimism and determination but they must have felt alone in their beliefs and hopes in deepest Essex.

Barely two years later, by the time the Purleigh colony was beginning to show signs of failure, they were no longer alone in this part of the country. The example of Purleigh, noised abroad through *The New Order* and similar progressive journals, inspired others to try their hands at community life. The depressed state of prices for agricultural land in the area meant that others also looked in this direction to set up their own experiments.

As early as 1895 James Evans, a member of the original Brotherhood Church in Southgate Road, Hackney and another follower of Tolstoy's principles, had bought three acres of land with a four-roomed cottage in Ashingdon, near Hockley, fourteen miles south of Purleigh and across the River Crouch.[2] It seems to have been a somewhat casual affair: "the friends go down there to work when they can".[3] In the *Labour Annual* of 1897 he was still advertising for fellow-thinkers to join 'a small anarchist group'. How long it was active and how many fellow-thinkers he attracted to the site is unknown but Evans was there long enough to build himself a cottage which he called 'Brotherhood Cottage' – on an unmade track called 'The Chase' – and to begin to grow vegetables and keep goats.[4]

In that same 1897 edition of the *Labour Annual* another announcement of a planned colony appeared, this one to be located in the village of Downham, near Wickford, just ten miles south-east of Purleigh and therefore closer to London. Once again the Croydon Brotherhood Church lay at the root of a colony enterprise; the prime mover, Henry Power, was a member of the church. The site chosen was somewhat larger in size than Purleigh; there were 29 acres of land and three cottages. On 23 July 1898 (very soon after the Purleigh meeting which led to defections), 33 prospective colonists assembled there to view and approve the location. It was acquired for £700, according to one source bought with financial support from none other than Arnold Eiloart.[5] But in other ways this was a much more modest – or perhaps one might say, prudent – scheme than that at Purleigh. It had been conceived at a meeting in London, in the Central Vegetarian Restaurant in St Bride's Street, and was profiled as a 'Colony for City Men', recognising that many of the would-be colonists might wish or need to continue their working careers in London while trying to develop an alternative life at the end of a railway line which would take them to Wickford in less than an hour. This 'part-time' approach necessitated a less communistic approach to both land ownership and the sharing of labour. Unlike the Purleigh regime, each colonist would buy a plot of a few acres and work it independently as and when he could. There could be no specified requirement as to the amount of work each put in.

The prime movers were committed Tolstoyans and definitely saw the projected colony as an opportunity to live in line with his ideas. But it would not be heavily prescriptive; "Perfect freedom is the watchword of the colony", declared Power in *The New Order*. In fact he was positively apologetic about the relaxed code of the proposed colony: "It will not be on the same lines as the Purleigh Colony, for the members of this new group are not able to shake themselves so free from their commercial fetters, and to this extent fall short of the examples set by the more fearless brothers".[6] Could we read this, perhaps, as an early indication that the Tolstoyan purity of the agenda set by Kenworthy and the Purleigh colonists was already being regarded, at least in some sympathetic circles, as over-ambitious and perhaps too authoritarian?

Meanwhile, at Mayland, on the banks of a creek of the river Blackwater, some six miles east of Purleigh, another hopeful utopian had pitched his camp in 1897. This time influenced by Robert Blatchford's socialist polemic, *Merrie England*, still a best-seller four years after its first appearance, it was a Mancunian printer by the name of Thomas Smith who brought his wife and children south to escape the increasingly overcrowded city. His advertisements in the *Labour Annual* for fellow-colonists offered 'individualist ownership, tempered by voluntary co-operation', along the lines of Power's Downham venture. The early years of the colony were dogged by the all too familiar problems of unpreparedness and lack of knowledge of horticulture. Smith had to return to Manchester from time to time to work in his old trade so as to support his wife and children, left behind to work the land.

Eventually, however, he found a way to turn the holding into a successful unit by cultivating tomatoes intensively under glass. It was a far cry from the original colonist ideal but impressive enough to persuade the philanthropic American industrialist, Joseph Fels, into taking Smith on as the manager of a huge, 600-acre estate on nearby land which he bought in 1905 to provide the opportunity for the East End poor to take up smallholdings and benefit from Smith's advice. The printer from Manchester ended up with a Gold Medal from the Royal Horticultural Society for services to the industry – a far cry from those early years of struggle.[7]

While the Purleigh colonists would never come together again in the close intensity they had experienced in those few short months or years, the legacy of their colony experience remained with them long after the grass had grown over their painfully tilled soil. Many of the notions that underlay it and certainly the experience of its successes and failures were carried through into their later life experiences.

The concept of shared lives within a 'colony' survived most fully among those who had left Purleigh for Whiteway. Somewhere around eight of the Purleigh colonists moved to Gloucestershire to form the core of what would follow and develop, taking with them their experience of the strengths and weaknesses of the 'Purleigh experience'. Things in Whiteway did not take the course they had expected, the first shock coming when Sam Bracher, who had to a large degree been the prime mover in the 'breakaway movement' and whose promise of financial backing was intended to underpin the first months and years, decided at a crucial moment to change his plans and instead to set up home with Lottie Dunn in their own house at Sheepscombe, a short distance from the Whiteway lands. Out of conscience, he still gave over half of his funds to the colony but it led inevitably to a rapid recalculation of what would and would not be possible.

Laying a road at the Whiteway Colony, 1924

That the radical edge of the group survived this first practical difficulty was quickly manifested when a collective decision was made that, as an expression both of their freedom from the oppression of law and of their commitment to future shared interests, they would burn the hard-won title deeds to their newly secured land. It was a bold step and one which could have proved a hostage to fortune but, rather surprisingly, when the notion of the collective undocumented ownership of the Whiteway property was challenged at a Land Tribunal as late as 1955, it was upheld, the regular meetings of colonists being deemed the licensor of lands and the individual colonists the licensees.

In another very significant respect, however, the longevity of the colony could be put down to an early decision over the vexed question which had, in part at least, 'broken' Purleigh: that of equal input of labour. Within a short space of time, it became apparent at Whiteway that there were those who were happier taking a share of the fruits of the communal labour than they were contributing fairly to the burden of work. In 1901 a collective decision was taken to allocate individual plots of land to individual colonists. Their very survival would then depend on their own efforts. It was a major shift from the philosophy of both Purleigh and the early months of Whiteway. Nevertheless, it seems to have had the desired effect and those less willing to work soon drifted away.

Their openness to evolution almost certainly accounts for the fact of Whiteway's longevity. The Whiteway colony survives to this day as a name, with well over a hundred residents, still with its monthly meeting for decisions on matters of import to the community as a whole. Now, however, each owns his or her property outright and most live or work outside the colony. For the founding settlers of 1898, this would have been the palest shadow of their ambitions.

At least three of the 'breakaway group' – William Sinclair, Jeannie Straughan and Nellie Shaw (who became the colony's biographer) – lived out the rest of their days in Whiteway. Another of the earliest Purleigh pioneers, William Sudbury Protheroe, stayed until he was 60, then moved to Salisbury to open a shop selling sweets and vegetarian food. In 1955, when he was 82, his West Indian wife told a reporter that he had become disillusioned with colony life: "Now the colony is just another hamlet. Its ideals have been swept away with the times".[8] He died in 1955.

Others had moved on, taking their idealism into different areas. Bracher, a Quaker and a journalist, found a new purpose during the 1st World War, turning his energies to the production of anti-War pamphlets. A fellow Quaker, Joseph Burtt, left Whiteway to tend his ailing father but in 1906 was recruited by William Cadbury (another Quaker) to go to west Africa to assess how far the cocoa beans from which Cadbury's chocolate products were manufactured were being harvested using slave labour. Burtt's damning report had a profound effect on the future conduct of the industry.[9] Eiloart, who had entered into a free union with May Pinnell of the Croydon Brotherhood, left after only a few months, though he returned from time to time for some years. He moved around, living fairly basically; in 1908 he was living in a tent at Long Ditton in Surrey with his wife and five children and paying his way by writing and lecturing on health, advocating nutrition as the key to well-being.[10] In 1927, when he was in his mid-sixties, he regularised his marriage to May but soon afterwards was admitted to a mental hospital outside Basingstoke where he died in 1932. Shortly before his death, he commented to Nellie Shaw that "idealism is, I fear, too often just a selfish egotism and, like patriotism, is not enough".[11]

For at least one Purleigh man, the unforeseen entry of the Doukhobors into the life of the colony led to a completely new direction in his life. Herbert Archer, who had been for a while Secretary to the Croydon Brotherhood and had then moved to Purleigh, became entangled with their cause and sailed to Canada. He was there to greet the S.S. 'Lake Huron' when it arrived carrying the first shipment of

Doukhobors from the Caucasus and remained with them in the difficult years as they sought to settle and be accepted in their new lands in northern Saskatchewan. He taught English and supported them as best he could until his untimely demise in 1906, burnt to death accidentally in his log cabin.[12]

That other hero of the Doukhobor cause, Arthur St. John, probably returned from Canada some time in 1899. His work on their behalf had so far taken him to the Caucasus, to Turkey by way of a Russian prison, to Cyprus and thence to Canada. No-one had been more assiduous in the practical help he had given them and he remained a loyal advocate when many others had become impatient with their intransigence in their new settlements. On his return to England he was a frequent lecturer, both on the Doukhobors and on other matters of concern to him, vegetarianism and non-resistance among them. In 1901, he went with Kenworthy on a visit to Tolstoy in Russia and later followed him into a journalistic venture in Wolverhampton (of which more later). He became increasingly interested in the issue of crime and penal reform and was a prime mover behind the formation, in 1907, of the Penal Reform League, set up to investigate the treatment of criminals and initiate a debate on the methods of punishment then in use. He became its first secretary and spoke and wrote on penal issues over the following years. In 1911 he was part of a campaigning group which founded a Women's Training Colony outside Newbury for the reform of prostitutes. During the War, adhering to his pacifist views, he volunteered for the Ambulance Corps. He eventually retired to Scotland but, keeping his idealism to the end, finished a utopian novel *Why Not Now?: A British Islander's Dream* in his final months. It was published posthumously in 1939. Croydon and Purleigh had been but brief stepping-stones in a life dedicated to humanitarian goals but they had no doubt played their part in developing his beliefs.

William Hone was, in many ways, the most 'grounded' of the colonists. Recruited as a practical horticulturalist, he had provided the backbone of the colony's working activity while remaining healthily sceptical of those who slavishly followed Tolstoy's dogma to the exclusion of concern for the economic viability of the enterprise. "Much time spent in meditation coupled with vague or visionary ideas that somehow things will come out all right will never accomplish much in the direction of building up Colonies. Meditation is doubtless good in its proper proportion to other duties", he had written in *The New Order* in November 1898, while the colony was disintegrating. The last to leave, he eventually took his family away from the scene of his toils, now slowly slipping back to nature. He was still there in 1910, living in Colony House, but by 1911 he could be found in south Suffolk, at Rooksey Green, outside Lavenham, where he described himself as 'florist, plant and fruit grower'.[13]

Others from the colony found that, even though things had not worked out as they had hoped or expected, their experience of working the land had equipped them for further ventures in horticulture. Hubert Hammond, by 1901, was living with a new wife and young baby in Mayland, just a few miles away to the east. He described himself to the census enumerator as a market gardener, as did Arthur Drover, in Great Baddow, to the west of Purleigh. Both had arrived – through, but not at Purleigh – at their goal of taking up an independent life away from the city, 'back to the land'.

The three Purleigh men closest to Tolstoy – Maude, Tchertkoff and Kenworthy – took a while to disentangle their lives one from the others. Each had met Tolstoy, each was devoted to him, his philosophy and his writings and was keen to sustain a relationship with him. Perhaps this was why the blame for the failure of the colony was passed around among them like a hot potato. There can be no doubt that all three wished to continue to promulgate Tolstoy's thought in Britain and were dedicated to that cause, but it was in the issue of who should do this and how that there was room for further antagonism.

Back in 1896, when Kenworthy had visited Tolstoy in Russia, he had come back convinced that he had returned with a commission to publish the first English translations of all Tolstoy's subsequent works through the medium of the Croydon Brotherhood Publishing Company. It was Tchertkoff himself who had drawn up the letter of confirmation. This agreement was deemed a great privilege by Kenworthy but it also had a practical value in that it would produce a useful income stream for the Brotherhood Church. Thus far all was well. But on closer examination there were limitations. The agreement only covered the first edition in Britain of any translation of Tolstoy's work. It also only covered future works; there had already been English language translations of, for example, *Anna Karenina* and *The Kingdom of God is Within You*. Furthermore, this limitation in favour of the Brotherhood Church was potentially in conflict with Tolstoy's more regularly expressed desire that his works should be freely available to the world, unconstrained by copyright. Though the Brotherhood Publishing Company would go on to publish at least ten of Tolstoy's titles, exclusivity was hard to maintain. When, for example, *War and Peace* appeared in 1897 in a new translation by the American Nathan Haskell Dole it was published by the firm of Walter Scott.

Maude would later go on to claim that Tolstoy had no recollection of the commitment he had given to Kenworthy, and indeed it is true that, over the succeeding years, Tolstoy had granted very similar concessions to Maude and to Tchertkoff, leaving each convinced of a special status and setting the scene for internecine warfare.[14] The pot was stirred still further when, in 1898, Kenworthy had handed over control of *The New Order* and of the Brotherhood Publishing Co. to Frank Henderson, formerly the manager of Brotherhood House in Croydon but also sometime employee of the radical Newcastle publisher, Walter Scott, who had, in the 1880s, published a number of Tolstoy's works, including the first English edition of *War and Peace*. Maude himself, while he was at Wickham's Farm, had translated *What is Art?* (1898) and *Stop and Think* (1899) for Henderson at the Brotherhood Publishing Company and, more significantly, Louise, his wife, placed her translation of the novel *Resurrection* in their hands in 1900. But that was the last they did for the Brotherhood. They parted company acrimoniously, accusing Henderson of misappropriating the royalties of *Resurrection* which Tolstoy had written specifically to help fund the resettlement of the Doukhobors.[15] The company effectively came to an end, taking with it *The New Order*, the last edition of which appeared in November 1901. Henderson went off to establish his own independent publishing house. To compound matters, Tchertkoff took offence at some of the wording in the Resurrection Fund's Annual Report for 1900-1 which, he claimed, underplayed and misstated his role in the Doukhobor affair. Despite a retraction in the following Report, this episode effectively brought to an end what had already become a difficult relationship between the former neighbours in Purleigh.[16] Pamphlets were written, legal action was threatened. Matters dragged on and eventually came to nothing.

Maude and his wife were now deeply engaged in what was to prove to be their life's work, of translating Tolstoy's writings. Thereafter, their ever-increasing cascade of translations, culminating in the great 1928 centenary edition of Tolstoy's works, was published through a range of publishers both in Britain and in America. They left Wickham's Farm in 1901 and moved to Great Baddow, outside Chelmsford, living in what one Russian visitor described as a dacha, built by

Aylmer Maude in later years

them in the Russian style.[17] Lodging with them was former colonist, Arthur Drover (now described as a market gardener) and his new wife Annie, sister of Lottie Dunn.[18]

While Maude's life remained firmly entwined with the work and thinking of Tolstoy, he turned, in the wake of the Purleigh experience, to support of more practical and less idealistic causes, in particular the co-operative movement and the Fabian Society, serving on its National Executive in the critical years when the Labour Party was beginning to make its mark in Parliament.

Tchertkoff had his own agenda in all this. Eager to spread the Tolstoyan word among the Russian community, both in Britain and back in Russia, he had been issuing a steady stream of Russian-language works, setting up his own press in

Purleigh and using the imprint Izdatel'stvo Svobodnago Slova (The Free Word Press).[19] Realising that there was a need and demand in Britain for English-language versions of some of these texts, he established a new imprint, the Free Age Press, and began, from 1900, to issue Tolstoy's shorter writings, in some cases and until their falling out, using Maude as translator. In this new venture, Tchertkoff recruited as his manager and joint editor, Arthur Fifield who, as well as having experience of the book trade had been functioning as the Secretary of the Croydon Brotherhood Church.

With both Fifield, the Church Secretary, and Henderson, the editor of *The New Order* and effective manager of the Brotherhood Publishing Company 'on board', a succession of Free Age Press publications began to appear with a Maldon or Purleigh imprint. They included titles which the Brotherhood Press had published only a year or two earlier. By the end of the year 1900, the whole operation was moved and the location of the publisher was given as Christchurch, Hants. Tchertkoff had left Purleigh for good and set up the press

Tolstoy with Tchertkoff in 1909

in Tuckton House on the south coast. With an entourage of employees and fellow émigrés he would remain there, issuing a string of Tolstoy's writings until he returned to Russia in 1908 to control Tolstoy's literary estate during his ailing years and after his death in 1910. He was still publishing titles when he died in 1936.

Finally, what of the later life of the prime instigator of the Purleigh venture, John Kenworthy? As we have seen, after the collapse of the first colony in 1898, Kenworthy continued to work with the Brotherhood Church wherever the sap still ran. He played an important role in the establishing of groups in both Leeds and Blackburn, meanwhile sustaining and participating as a regular lecturer in the programme of activities of the Tolstoyan Society in London which he had helped found in 1898.[20] As always, he busied himself with speaking and writing and always kept an eye on new ventures. In July 1900 he wrote, from the Grey House, to Alfred Russel Wallace, the evolutionist, social activist and spiritualist, setting out his idea of writing 'not so much a biography, but, strung upon a thread of the most necessary biographical fact, an ordered and measured statement of your work'. Wallace was not unsympathetic to the idea but managed skilfully to deflect him: "I really think you had better employ yourself in devoting all your powers to the main problem, of how to reform our rotten Social system which you have so forcibly described". The scheme came to nothing.[21]

That the break-up of the colony had affected him badly, however, we know from his own later account in *Tolstoy, His Life and Works*:

In the spring of this year [1901], finding that certain entanglements connected with the Purleigh Colony (which arose out of my work at the Brotherhood Church at Croydon) were strangling all my efforts, destroying my relations in literature, and wearing me down towards physical extinction, I felt myself compelled to break with the past associations, and begin anew. As a first step, I once more visited Tolstoy.[22]

He goes on to speak rapturously of the five days he spent with the Master, now aged 74 and ailing but unswerving in his commitments and beliefs.

It would be possible to read too much into a passage in Kenworthy's book which occurs a few pages before his account of this visit but it speaks a lot of the strain under which he felt himself to be:

> I find that the real, the complete, the awful sacrifice which the Christ-life demands is to live day by day, year by year, calculating all your acts to the equal welfare of every creature with yourself, and meanwhile to be accused of selfishness, by some, for doing it, and by others for not doing it.[23]

Is it too fanciful to see reflected in this the accusations of excessive control levelled against Kenworthy at the time of the break-up? And is it also too great a leap to connect Kenworthy's crisis with the emergence within him of a new, intensified strain of spiritual interest? As far back as 1885, following the death of his two infant daughters, Kenworthy had taken to exploring the literature of spiritualism. His brother's death in 1896 had turned his thoughts once again to the matter of some form of life after death.[24] Now, in April 1901, we find Kenworthy addressing a meeting of the London Spiritualist Alliance on the subject of 'My Psychic Experiences'. In the course of his talk he revealed "that he had been in communication with spirit entities who claimed to be Emerson and Morris, and found that, by following their counsel, success had come to him in various ways".[25] Three months later he was addressing the annual conference of the National Federation of Spiritualists in Sheffield.

This fascination with the spirit world had apparently been growing for some time. A year before, a note to Tchertkoff from Jane Holah (who, with her sister Florence, had been helping with his publishing work) had commented on a meeting in which, to her relief, 'Kenworthy had kept off spiritualism' – obviously contrary to her expectations. It was not unusual at the time for those committed to free thought to venture down this road. Among those who took an interest were the philosopher William James, the novelist Sir Arthur Conan Doyle, the eventual Prime Minister Arthur Balfour and the naturalist Alfred Russel Wallace, with whom Kenworthy was in correspondence. Nevertheless, we might perhaps see in Kenworthy's case, given the pressures which he clearly felt himself to be under, a welcome source of reassurance 'from the other side' as to his actions and beliefs.

Despite the turbulence in his mind, Kenworthy returned to England from Yasnaya Polyana with a new burst of energy. In June he wrote to the press soliciting public donations towards the publication of 'an orderly selection of Tolstoy's work, together with an adequate account of his life, so that his teaching may be easily grasped as a whole and as a system'. Cheques were to be made in favour of the Tolstoy Publishing Company, though the finished results were to be issued in due course by the Brotherhood Publishing Company.[26] The timing coincided almost exactly with the effective demise of that company. When Kenworthy's life of Tolstoy appeared in 1902, it appeared under the imprint of Walter Scott, Frank Henderson's old company.

Meanwhile he brought out, in quick succession, a third edition of his *Anatomy of Misery*, newly equipped with an introduction by Tolstoy, and *Book of Visions*, a collected edition of his own poetry, written over the course of the past two decades.[27] This was almost feverish activity.

Up until this point, though constantly travelling to lecture and sustain his contacts around the country, Kenworthy had retained his house in Purleigh. His sons were at school in the Quaker Friends School at Saffron Walden on the far side of Essex and, until the smallpox outbreak of 1901/2, he had the Blackburn Brotherhood group on hand on the colony site. In 1902, however, he embarked on a new and very different venture which took him to an entirely new location, to Bilston on the edge of Wolverhampton, a town built on steel-making and coal-mining. How Kenworthy came to be appointed to the post of editor of the *Midland Weekly Herald* is not clear but it seems likely that he was bent on using the platform of a provincial newspaper to spread his beliefs in an area where the effects of industrial capitalism were all too clear.

Very quickly he was in trouble. In May he was committed for trial at the Staffordshire Assizes for attempting to pervert the course of justice. A Wolverhampton man, a Poor Law Guardian, had been accused of 'an offence against morals' with another man and Kenworthy had weighed in in an editorial, accusing the police of 'being after' the defendant and hinting that the case had been rigged, perhaps because of his religious affiliations – the accused was a spiritualist. The case came to court in July and Kenworthy was found guilty. The jury took a lenient line and he was bound over but the incident found its way into the columns of newspapers all over the country.

That was just the start of an 'annus horribilis' for Kenworthy. The coronation of Edward VII was scheduled for

26 June but had to be postponed at the last moment while the king underwent surgery. The *Herald* carried an article that week by Kenworthy which was less than complimentary of the new king. The result was an angry mob which besieged his house, shouting and attempting to break down the door. Ironically, it was the police and they alone who kept him from being assaulted.[28]

In November 1902 Kenworthy was back in court, this time as plaintiff in a libel case against the *Sun* newspaper which, in an article under the headline 'Among the Anarchists – the gospel of the knife, revolver, torch and bomb', had named him as a potential danger in a paragraph headed 'Bomb Advocates as Editors'. The text of the article had explicitly referred to him as a 'Tolstoyan anarchist and a member of the Brotherhood Church', making the distinction between militant anarchists and those, like Kenworthy, who believed merely in the long-term and

Kenworthy in 1900

peaceably achieved goal of freedom from governmental 'oppression'. The headlines, however, spoke less cautiously and blurred the distinction in the interests of attention-grabbing. In a year which saw attempts on the lives of the kings of Italy and Belgium and police activity against anarchist cells across Europe, these were niceties of political belief which easily escaped the popular mind. Kenworthy lost his case.

He no doubt felt besieged and when the owner of the *Midland Herald* returned from a trip to the United States and distanced himself in print from the editor's expressed views, it marked the end of the road for Kenworthy's tenure.[29] The failure, in the following year, of his libel case against the *Daily News* (explored in the previous chapter) would have done nothing to reassure him.

Moreover, this was going on while the issue of the exclusive rights to publish Tolstoy's texts in English was growing increasingly heated. Kenworthy was now threatening to sue his former friend Maude if he did not stop publishing Tolstoy's texts under other imprints. Maude wrote to his literary agent, G.H. Perris: "You will be amused to hear that J.C. Kenworthy has served me with a writ claiming 'damages for libel, slander, attack upon intellectual status and security and improper interference with family and affairs'"[30]. It was bluster. For Kenworthy and for the Brotherhood Publishing Company it was simply too late. Whatever the validity of Tolstoy's commitment to that company back in 1896, it was clear that there was, by now, no effective means of containing the publishing energy of either Maude or Tchertkoff.

It was all too much for Kenworthy. In the spring of 1904 he effectively fled the country having left his editorial post in the Midlands. He sailed for New York with plans to meet up with another of Tolstoy's correspondents, Alonzo Hollister, living in the Shaker community in Mount Lebanon in Pennsylvania. By the time of his return, later in the year, the will to continue his life's work seems to have faded. He had lost contact with his daughter, Agnes, and seems to have spent some time trying to find her and restore good relations with her. In 1909, he suffered a mental collapse.

The circumstances were dramatic. On 24 November, he was taken to the Moot Hall, Maldon to be seen by Dr Henry Brown. Brown recorded what he heard while examining him:

He talks incoherently, about the wrongs inflicted upon himself as a grandson of King William IVth, by the Jews. He says that all the food in his house is poisoned with Borassic and Prussic acids. He says that he is informed by His Majesty the Sultan that all the Cocoa plantations have been poisoned by the Jews.

Frank Brand, a household servant employed by Mrs Kenworthy, was there to give evidence that Kenworthy slept

Agnes Kenworthy

with a hatchet by his bed and refused to eat for fear of poisoning and, furthermore, refused to allow his wife to eat.

Brown consigned him to the Essex Lunatic Asylum at Warley, near Brentwood.[31]

An unknown factor here is the state of his wife Eleanor's health at the time. By 1911 the census returns tell us that she was a patient in a private hospital in Kelvedon, some thirteen miles north of Purleigh. She never left, dying there in 1912 at the age of 56.[32] By the time she was admitted, Kenworthy had been transferred from Warley to Middlesbrough Asylum in Yorkshire. Later he would be moved again, to the West Yorkshire Pauper Lunatic Asylum at Stanley, near Wakefield.

Instrumental in bringing about these moves was a former Quaker and a member of the Leeds Brotherhood, Eliza Pickard. From the time of his removal to Yorkshire she continued to visit him and to look after his welfare until her death. She died in 1942, aged 84. It is hard not to read some significance into the fact that in the graveyard of the Quaker Burial Ground at Adel outside Leeds she is recorded as Eliza Pickard Kenworthy; what precisely that significance is, however, we may not ever discover.[33]

Kenworthy seems to have spent the last decades of his life passing in and out of mental institutions. At times family records give a glimpse of his movements; he was able to attend the wedding of his son, Fred, in 1917 and he was in

Kenworthy (back row, right) at the wedding of his son, Fred, in 1917

Birkenhead in 1928 following the death of his sister, Amelia.[34] His social and political activities, however, seem to have been long – and irreversibly – abandoned. He ended his days back in an asylum, the Bootham Park Hospital in York, on 13 September 1948. He was 87 years old.[35]

By the time Kenworthy died a half century had passed since the abandonment by the first colonists of the Purleigh experiment. Tolstoyism, despite its influence on later figures and movements (and in particular on Gandhi's doctrine of

Tolstoy with his disciple, Mahatma Gandhi

passive resistance) had become largely a distant memory. Much of the passion stirred by his writings during the 1890s had been absorbed into other movements, other directions. At its height in the early and mid–1890s, Tolstoy's writings had spawned apostles in Russia, Europe and America. The numbers may have been small but the enthusiasm had been real, even passionate. Lectures had been given and journals had been started up to spread the word and establish connections. In the Netherlands colonies had been set up, as at Purleigh, to live out versions of the Tolstoyan ideal. The big Christian Commonwealth colony set up in 1896 in Georgia in America and covering nearly a thousand acres, though not specifically Tolstoyan, shared his Christian Socialist goals. It collapsed in 1900, a financial failure, its end marred by a flurry of law suits and recriminations.[36] The Dutch colony of the

Tolstoyan 'International Brotherhood' had come and gone; its life-span was even shorter than Purleigh's.[37] Even the most celebrated and influential community of all those based upon Tolstoy's thinking, Gandhi's Tolstoy Farm, outside Johannesburg, which became the heart of his passive resistance movement, lasted only from 1910 to 1913.[38] *The New Order* had long since ceased publication, as had its German and Hungarian equivalents.[39] In Gloucestershire, at the Whiteway community, the founding principles had been slowly watered down with the passage of time. In Yorkshire the Leeds Brotherhood Church, translated to a rural site at Stapleton outside Pontefract in 1921, was alive and persists to this day. In 2016 there were only four residents who, though the tenets of their way of life would have been recognisable to and approved by Tolstoy, do not feel in any sense bound by his principles.[40]

At Purleigh there are few traces of the colony to be found today. In Hackman's Lane stands a neat white house with bay windows and a tiled roof, set in a tidy garden behind an elegant railing. It bears the name-plate Colony House and

'Colony House' as it is today

The enlarged 'Grey House', seen in 2018

certainly sits square on the former colony land. Is it possible that within this, now much enlarged and altered, lie the vestiges of the brick house which cost the early colonists so much hard labour to build? Across the road and a little to the north the Grey House still stands, though now raised from its original single storey. Within the colony plot, new buildings and new enterprises have been added and only the boundaries of the orchard plot can be identified by thick hedges. When the Ordnance Survey came to revise its mapping of the site in the 1920s the orchard was still intact as was one of the long greenhouses. Now they are long gone.

With the exception of the Hadleigh Farm colony, set up and run by the Salvation Army, the various colonies, of differing complexions and purposes, which grew up around southern Essex have all, likewise, come and gone, each with its own initial goals and ambitions and each with its own complex history of success and failure. It would be hard to claim any kind of uniqueness for Purleigh though it was, without doubt, one of the most ambitious experiments of its kind at the time and, partly because of the very effective publicity it received among like-minded people across the country, both through the press and through the pages of *The New Order*, its progress was widely watched. As we have seen, the experience of being part of that experiment markedly affected the later lives of many of its colonists. "No disillusionment, I believe, caused any Purleigh immigrant to lament the upheaval which that search for rightness of life had meant; indeed, for one or two it was a valuable beginning": that was Percy Redfern's conclusion.[41] The evidence suggests that it was many more than one or two who were affected in the conduct of their later lives by the Purleigh experience.

The model which Purleigh provided was one from which later experiments would benefit, either by following or modifying the principles and practices put in place there.

Even the inadequacies and failings of the colony were put to use as warnings of traps to be avoided. Though its lifetime was short, the shadow it cast was long. The grass, it is true, grew quickly over the colony soil, so patiently won foot by foot, but the idealism which powered every lift and strike of the spade was carried forward to other ventures and passed on by those who had shared those months of comradeship and labour.

The last words should perhaps go to Kenworthy himself:

The revolution will not come thus heroically. Ours is the day of small things; of spreading abroad the new spirit; of uniting our men and women; of framing and executing plans of business organisation; of reducing principles and preaching to complete practice in our deeds. Yet out of small things, the great shall come; who can say, how soon? [42]

Appendix I

CONSTITUTION OF THE PURLEIGH COLONY, 1899

Articles of Constitution of the Brotherhood Colony, Purleigh, Essex.[1]

Friends who think of getting back to the land in co-operation with others will be interested to read the Purleigh Constitution, now printed for the first time.

1. The objects are to form a colony for carrying on Agriculture and other pursuits as far as may be on Communal lines.

2. The Colony-land shall be vested in a Trustee or Trustees, who shall be controlled by the colonists, by unanimous vote.[2]

3. The first Colonists shall be (etc., etc., etc.) and such others as may be admitted as Colonists as herein provided.

4. The Colonists may depute any powers and duties to any one or more of their number, and may elect such officers as they deem necessary, and they shall appoint a Secretary and a Treasurer.

5. The Secretary shall conduct the business on behalf of the Colony with outsiders: and where necessary, with individual colonists; contracts shall be signed by him on behalf of the Colony and countersigned by the Treasurer.

6. The Treasurer shall be responsible for the common funds, and may make payments and give receipts.

7. Any private personal property of any new Colonist may remain his, but if he desires any articles or things which he allows to be used by the other Colonists, or to be mixed with Colony property to remain his own, he must lodge a Schedule and Declaration to that effect with the Secretary otherwise he will be considered to have given them to the Colony.

8. In case any Colonist is dissatisfied, or for any reason

wishes to withdraw or retire from the Colony, he may enter into an Agreement with the Secretary that he shall receive the sum that he shall have paid into the common funds, and his own personal property and such sum shall be payable by instalments as the Secretary may, with the approbation of the other Colonists, arrange, and upon the making of such agreement his rights as a Colonist shall cease.

9. Failing such agreement being made, the retiring Colonist may call upon the Secretary to assign him a portion of the land, whereupon the Secretary shall parcel out the Colony land (exclusive of Building Plots) into as many Plots, equal in area as there are Colonists; and shall assign to the retiring Colonist such plot as the Colonists may determine.

10. The Trustee or Trustees shall thereupon, at the request of the Secretary, grant the retiring Colonist a lease for his life of such plot at a peppercorn or nominal rent, containing the following stipulations, or such of them that the Secretary may direct.

> a) That the plot leased is for the personal enjoyment of the lessee, and shall not descend to his heirs or next of kin, nor be assigned or sublet by him, unless with the consent of the Secretary first obtained in writing; and that in case of the lessee's death or bankruptcy; or the taking of the same in execution for the lessee's debts, the term shall cease, and the plot shall revert back to the Trustee or Trustees for the benefit of the Colonists.

> b) The retiring Colonist shall have rights of way over all recognised roads and footpaths of the Colony-land and similarly the other Colonists shall have rights of way over all recognised roads and footpaths over the plot of the retiring Colonist, and no fencing shall be erected in derogation of this right.

> c) The retiring Colonist shall pay his fair share of rates and taxes and tithes in respect of his plot to the Secretary on the same becoming due. And the

Secretary's apportionment shall be final and binding.

d) In case the retiring Colonist shall for the space of 12 months cease to cultivate his plot he shall be considered to have surrendered it to the Trustee or Trustees for the benefit of the Colony.

11. Upon the granting of such lease, all the rights of the retiring Colonist in common lands and common money, goods, crops and effects shall cease, but he shall be entitled to the exclusive use of the crops upon his plot so ascertained.

12. In the absence of any definite arrangement to the contrary, the maintenance of a Colonist shall be deemed an equivalent for his services.

13. All proposing Colonists shall be admitted only on the unanimous vote of the then existing Colonists and they shall subscribe to the foregoing articles on being admitted. Colonists who do not attend the meeting at which such vote is taken shall be communicated with by the Secretary and invited to vote on the admission of such Colonist, and in the absence of a response within 14 days of the posting or making of such communication, they shall be deemed to vote in favour of such proposed Colonist.

14. The above articles shall be only altered at a special meeting to be called for the purpose and 14 days' notice of the proposed alteration shall be given or sent to each Colonist, and the vote of those present must be unanimous.

Christian, R.F. (ed.): *Tolstoy's Letters*, Vol. II, 1880-1910, London, 1976

Fish, J.O.: 'The Christian Commonwealth Colony: a Georgia Experiment, 1896-1900', *The Georgia Historical Quarterly*, Vol. 57, No.2, 1973, pp.213-226.

Hardy, D: *Alternative Communities in Nineteenth Century England*, London, 1979

Hardy, D. and Ward, C.: *Arcadia for All: The Legacy of a Makeshift Landscape*, Nottingham, 2004

Higgins, A.G.: *History of the Brotherhood Church*, Stapleton, 1982

Higgs, Catherine: *Cocoa, Slavery and Colonial Africa*, Ohio, 2012

Hocking, Salome: *Belinda the Backward: a Romance of Modern Idealism*, London, 1905

Holman, M.J. de K., 'The Purleigh Colony: Tolstoyan Togetherness in the Late 1890s' in Jones, M.: *New Essays on Tolstoy*, Cambridge, 1978

Holman, M.J. de K.: 'Translating Tolstoy for the Free Age Press: Vladimir Chertkov and His English Manager Arthur Fifield', *Slavonic and East European Review*, Vol. 66 No.2, April 1988

Horsbrugh-Porter, Anna: *Memories of Revolution: Russian Women Remember*, New York, 1993

Jones, P. d'A.: *The Christian Socialist Revival, 1877-1914*, London, 1968

Kelvin, N.: *The Collected Letters of William Morris*, Princeton, 1984-1996

Kenworthy, J.C.: *The Judgment of the City, and Other Poems* and Verses, London, 1889

Kenworthy, J.C.: *Amgiad and the Fair Lady, and Other Poems*, London, 1893

Kenworthy, J.C.: *The Anatomy of Misery: Plain Lectures on Economics*, London, 1893

Kenworthy, J.C.: *Christian Revolt*, London, 1893

Kenworthy, J.C.: *From Bondage to Brotherhood: an Address to the Workers*, London, 1894

Kenworthy, J.C.: *Pilgrimage to Tolstoy*, Croydon, 1896

Kenworthy, J.C.: *The World's Last Passage*, London, 1896

Kenworthy, J.C.: *Tolstoy, His Life and Works*, London and Newcastle, 1902

Marsh, J.: *Back to the Land: The Pastoral Impulse in Victorian England from 1880 to 1914*, London, 1982

Maude, A.: *Tolstoy and his Problems: Essays*, London, 1901

Maude, A.: *A Peculiar People: The Doukhobors*, London, 1904

Maude, A.: *The Life of Tolstoy*, Vol.1, *The First Fifty Years*, London, 1908; Vol.2, *The Later Years*, London, 1911

Maude, A.: 'Recollections of Tolstoy', *Slavonic and East European Review*, Vol.7, No.20, 1929

Morris, W.: *News from Nowhere, or An Epoch of Rest: Being Some Chapters from a Utopian Romance*, London, 1890

Muggeridge, M.: *Chronicles of Wasted Time*, London, 1972

Osgood, Kelsey: 'Life at One of England's Last Tolstoyan Communes', *The New Yorker*, 6 Jan. 2016

Peaker, Carol L.: 'Reading Revolution: Russian Emigrés and the Reception of Russian Literature in England, c.1890–1905', unpublished thesis, Wolfson College, Oxford, 2006

Popoff, A.: *Tolstoy's False Disciple,* New York, 2014

Potter, S.: *Purleigh's Past in Old Photographs*, 2nd. edn., Purleigh, 2007

Pringle, R.H.: *Supplement to the Report on Ongar, Chelmsford, Maldon and Braintree Districts of Essex*. Royal Commission on Agricultural Depression, 1894

Redfern, P.: *Journey to Understanding*, London, 1946

Roberts, Jason L.: 'The Ruin of Rural England: an Interpretation of Late 19th-Century Agricultural Depression, 1879-1914', unpublished thesis, Loughborough University, 1997

Ruskin, J.: *Fors Clavigera: Letters to the Workmen and Labourers of Great Britain*, London, 1871-1884

Scotland, N.: *Squires in the Slums: Settlements and Missions in Late-Victorian London*, New York, 2007

Shaw, N.: *Whiteway: a Colony on the Cotswolds*, London, 1935

Smiles, S.: *Self-Help, with Illustrations of Character and Conduct,* 1859

Tchertkoff, V.: *Christian Martyrdom in Russia: Persecution of the Spirit-Wrestlers (or Doukhoborski) in the Caucasus*, Croydon, 1897

Thacker, J.: *Whiteway Colony: The Social History of a Tolstoyan Community*, Stroud, 1993

Wallace, J. B.: *Towards Fraternal Organisation: an Explanation of the Brotherhood Trust*, 4th. edn., London, 1895

Webber, R.: 'The printer who came back to the land', *Essex Countryside*, Vol.23, No.221, June 1975

Woodcock, G.: 'Russian Writers and the Doukhobors' in *Slavic and East-European Connections,* a special issue of *Canadian Literature*, 120, Spring 1989

Woodcock, G and Avakumovic, I: *The Doukhobors*, Toronto, 1968

SERIAL PUBLICATIONS

Brotherhood: [journal of the Brotherhood Church], Limavady and London, 1887-1932

Croydon Brotherhood Intelligencer, The: Croydon, 1895 [continued as *The New Order*]

Labour Annual, The: A Year-Book of Industrial Progress and Social Welfare, Manchester, 1895-1900

New Order, The: Croydon and Purleigh, 1895-1901

Seed-Time: [journal of the Fellowship of the New Life], Kingston-on-Thames, 1889-1898

ON-LINE SOURCES

Draper, Christopher: 'From Everton to the Asylum (1861-1948)', 2016, on the *Northern Voices* website: (http://northernvoicesmag.blogspot.com/2016/09/from-everton-to-asylum-1861-1948.html)

NOTES

INTRODUCTION

[1]   Booth, Charles: *Life and Labour of the People*, 1889. Booth's much expanded second edition appeared in nine volumes, between 1892 and 1897 under the title *Life and Labour of the People in London.*

[2]   Marsh, J.: *Back to the Land: The Pastoral Impulse in Victorian England from 1880 to 1914*, 1982, p.2.

[3]   A good guide to these progressive manifestations is Marsh, J.: *op. cit.*, 1982.

[4]   For a detailed assessment of this movement see Marsh, Jan: *op.cit.*, 1982, Hardy, D.: *Alternative Communities in Nineteenth-Century England*, 1979 and Armytage, W.H.G.: *Heavens Below: Utopian Experiments in England, 1560-1960*, 1961.

[5]   Hardy, D.: *Alternative Communities in Nineteenth Century England*, 1979

Chapter 1
THE GROUNDWORK

[1]   Kenworthy was married to Eleanor Emily Robinson in 1883 in Birkenhead. There were five children. Gertrude and Hilda died in infancy; Emily Agnes was born in 1886; John Frederick in 1888; George Clive in 1890.

[2]   Ruskin, J: *Fors Clavigera* I, V, 23.

[3]   The Liverpool Society was part of a network, with branches also in Birmingham, Manchester and Aberdeen. They engaged in civic and social reform activities, as well as reading and discussion. Kenworthy, writing in his *Tolstoy: His Life and Works*, 1902, p.12, claimed to have met Ruskin seventeen years previously.

[4]   This according to an autobiographical note in *The Labour Annual* for 1895, p.177.

5   Kenworthy, J.C.: *op. cit.*, 1902, p.212.

6   Jones, P. d'A.: *The Christian Socialist Revival, 1877-1914*, p.315. Kelvin, N. (ed.): *The Collected Letters of William Morris, Vol. 3, 1889-1892.* Kenworthy would be in touch with Morris on several further occasions. In 1892, while in America, he would send him a copy of his newly published volume of poems *Amgiad and the Fair Lady,* and would attempt, unsuccessfully, to persuade him to cross the Atlantic to give some lectures.

7   Kenworthy, J.C.: *op. cit.*, 1902, p.213.

8   Kenworthy, J.C.: *op. cit.*, 1902, pp.212-4.

9   Kenworthy, J.C.: *op. cit.*, 1902, p.12. The title *What To Do?* was retranslated in later editions as *What Then Must We Do?* and *What Is To Be Done?*

10   Kenworthy, J.C.: *op. cit.*, 1902, p.12.

11   Passenger list of S.S. 'Adriatic' (www.ancestry.co.uk). A report in the *Essex County Chronicle*, 12 November 1897, claimed that Kenworthy was on his way to run a bacon factory in America. This seems to be borne out by another statement, in *The Rocket*, that he was 'at one time in the frozen meat trade'.

12   I am grateful to Stephanie Philpotts for this information.

13   Kenworthy, J.C.: *Pilgrimage to Tolstoy,* Brotherhood Publishing Co., 1896, reprinted in T*olstoy: His Life and Work*, 1902, p.47.

14   An undated letter to Kenworthy from Morris in Kelvin, N. (ed.): *The Collected Letters of William Morris, Vol. 3, 1889-1892,* p.155.

15   In particular Kenworthy cites his story, *The Kreutzer Sonata,* which first appeared in English translation in both America and Britain in 1890.

16   Kenworthy, J.C.:*op. cit.*, 1902, p.13.

17   Passenger list of S.S. 'Mississippi' (www.ancestry.co.uk).

[18] On Mansfield House, see Scotland, N.: *Squires in the Slums: Settlements and Missions in Late-Victorian London*, 2007.

[19] *Morning Post*, 20 October 1893.

[20] *The Anatomy of Misery* was published by the radical publisher, William Reeves, in 1893. It was republished two years later under the imprint of the newly created Brotherhood Publishing Company. Kenworthy had already, in 1889, published two volumes of verses, *The Judgment of the City, and other poems and verses* in 1889 and *Amgiad and the Fair Lady, and other poems*, written in America in 1891 but published only in 1893.

[21] Kenworthy, J.C.: *The Anatomy of Misery*, 1895, p.96.

[22] Kenworthy, J.C.: *op. cit.*, 1895, p.98.

[23] *Seed-Time*, January 1896; cited in Armytage, W.H.G.: 'J.C. Kenworthy and the Tolstoyan Communities in England' in *American Journal of Economics And Sociology, Vol. 16, No. 4*, July 1957.

[24] Wallace had been born in Gujerat, India, the son of a Presbyterian minister. He had studied theology at Belfast, Dublin and Bonn and become a Congregational minister but had turned to Socialism around 1885, having been persuaded by Henry George's advocacy of a single tax on land, and resigned his ministry. He retired to Limavady, where he began his magazine, *Brotherhood*. In 1889 he moved to Belfast and began the *Socialist Evening Star*. He came to London in 1891 after visiting a number of colonies in north and central America, including A.K. Owen's recently founded utopian colony in Topolobampo, Mexico (autobiographical note in *The Labour Annual*, 1895).

[25] *Towards Fraternal Organisation: an Explanation of the Brotherhood Trust*, 4th edn. 1895, p.2.

Chapter 2
The Brotherhood Ideal

[1]   The manifesto survives in an undated pamphlet, *Towards Fraternal Organisation: an Explanation of the Brotherhood Trust*, by J. Bruce Wallace, which went through a number of editions, later under the title *Preparing for the Twentieth Century*.

[2]   Wallace, J. Bruce: *op. cit.*, 4th edn., 1895, p.17.

[3]   *The Surrey County Reporter*, 16 June 1894.

[4]   Shaw, N.: *Whiteway: a Colony on the Cotswolds*, 1935, p.20.

[5]   *The Croydon Brotherhood Intelligencer* of January 1895 names the Committee as Grover, Shaw, Muggeridge, William Gilruth, and James and Frank Henderson. N. Shaw, *op. cit.*, 1935, p.26, however, recalls the pioneering group as consisting of Grover, Shaw, G.D. Blogg, William Swainson and a married couple, the Frazers. Malcolm Muggeridge's autobiography, *Chronicles of Wasted Time* (1972) gives a graphic picture of a childhood in a socialist household in Croydon.

[6]   Earlier writers on the Brotherhood Church have assumed they bought the premises, but a letter by the then Secretary, Herbert Archer, published 17 October 1896 in the *Croydon Chronicle*, makes it clear that this was not so.

[7]   Shaw, N.: *op. cit.*, 1935, p.21.

[8]   *Croydon Advertiser*, 16 June 1894.

[9]   Kenworthy writes, in *Pilgrimage to Tolstoy*, 1896, that there were four or five score who attended.

[10]   Hocking, S.: *Belinda the Backward: a Romance of Modern Idealism*, 1905, p.74.

[11]   Shaw, N.: *op.cit.*, 1935, p.21.

[12]   *The Croydon Brotherhood Intelligencer*, Vol.I, No.1, Jan. 1895.

[13]   *The New Order*, Vol.III, No.10, September 1897.

[14]   *The New Order*, Vol.III, No.10, Sept. 1897. The Rational Dress Society had been founded in 1881.

15   *The New Order*, Vol.II, No.11, November 1896.

16   *The Croydon Brotherhood Intelligencer*, Vol.I, No.1, Jan. 1895.

17   *The Croydon Brotherhood Intelligencer*, Vol.1, No.10, Oct. 1895.

18   Alston, C: *Tolstoy and his Disciples*, p.91.

19   *The Croydon Brotherhood Intelligencer*, Vol.1, No.3, March 1895.

20   To judge from the pages of subsequent issues, however, there is little evidence that these materialised.

21   On the Starnthwaite Colony, see Hardy, D: *op.cit.*, 1979, pp.111-4.

22   Shaw, N.: *op. cit.*, 1935, p.27.

23   *The New Order*, Vol.I, No.11, November 1895.

24   *The Croydon Brotherhood Intelligencer*, Vol.1, No.3, March 1895.

25   Bartlett, R.: *Tolstoy, a Russian Life*, 2010, p.362.

26   The text of Tolstoy's letter is transcribed in Christian, R.F. (ed.): *Tolstoy's Letters*, Vol. II, 1880-1910, 1978, p.522.

27   Tchertkoff's name is frequently spelt Chertkov in English-language publications. I have used the form he himself used in his English works.

28   Kenworthy, J.C.: 'Pilgrimage to Tolstoy' in *Tolstoy: His Life and Work*, 1902, p.98.

29   *Brotherhood*, New Series 3:11, March 1896, cited in Alston, C. *op. cit.*, p.254, n.14.

30   The text of the letter confirming this and drafted by Tchertkoff is to be found in the edition of Tolstoy's letters edited by R.F. Christian, Vol.2, p.534. It is quoted in full in Popoff, A.: *Tolstoy's False Disciple*, 2014, p.122.

31   The text of this letter appears in Kenworthy, J.C.: *op. cit.*, 1902, p.242 et seq.

32   Baker would subsequently go on to take Wallace's place at the Brotherhood Church in Southgate Road, Hackney and,

still later, became pastor of the Congregational Church in Truro, Cornwall.

[33] *The New Order,* Vol.II, No.3, March 1896.

[34] *The New Order*, Vol.II, No.8, August 1895.

[35] At the time of the 1891 census, Purleigh had 858 inhabitants.

[36] Kelly's *Directory of Essex*, 1898.

[37] Pringle, R.H.: Supplement to the Report on Ongar, Chelmsford, Maldon and Braintree Districts of Essex. *Royal Commission on Agricultural Depression,* 1894.

[38] *Royal Commission on Agriculture Depression. Final Report* (Cmnd 8540), 1897.

[39] On the effects of the depression in Essex, see Chapter 4 of 'The Ruin of Rural England: an Interpretation of Late 19th-Century Agricultural Depression, 1879-1914', an unpublished thesis by Jason L. Roberts, Loughborough University, 1997.

[40] Nunn described himself in the electoral registers of the time and in Kelly's *Directory* of 1899 as 'land agent'.

[41] I am grateful to Steven Potter of Purleigh for sight of the plan of this proposed development.

[42] For an overview of these plot-sales in Essex, see Hardy, D. and Ward. C.: *Arcadia for All,* 2004, pp.115-164.

[43] *Essex County Chronicle,* 28 March 1898.

[44] *Essex County Chronicle,* 19 Nov. and 13 Dec. 1897.

[45] *The New Order,* Vol.II, No.6, June 1896.

[46] Sinclair's 'approximate statement of the funds of Purleigh Colony', dated 1912, is in Leeds University Library, Special Collections: LRA: MS1380/1832. It is reproduced as Appendix II. Whether based on Sinclair's memory or written record it is not possible to say.

[47] *The New Order,* Vol.II, No.9, Sept. 1896.

Chapter 3
BACK TO THE LAND

[1] Cold Norton Station, opened in 1889 on a new branch line from Woodham Ferrers to Maldon, was closed to passengers in 1939.

[2] Reported in *The Clarion*, 28 Aug., 1898.

[3] *The New Order,* Vol.III, No.3, March 1897.

[4] Shaw, N: *op. cit.*, 1935, p.32.

[5] See Appendix II.

[6] *The New Order*,Vol.III, No.4, April 1897.

[7] *The New Order*,Vol.III, No.4, April 1897.

[8] Hocking, S.: *op. cit.*, p.160. Although a fictional account, there can be no doubt that this was based on the author's personal experience of the colony.

[9] *Essex County Chronicle* report, 2 April 1897, in the Cuttle Collection of newscuttings, Essex Record Office T/P 181/8/42.

[10] N. Shaw, *op. cit.*, 1935, p.32.

[11] I owe this knowledge to Steven Potter, who drew my attention to the Geological Survey of Great Britain, Solid and Draft Edition map of 1975: Sheet 241, Chelmsford.

[12] The experienced brickmaker may have been Peter Harkin who, in the 1901 census for Purleigh was aged 70 and living with his wife in Hackman's Road, next door to the Hones. He is described there as a brickburner, born in Scotland

[13] *Essex County Chronicle*, 12 Nov. 1897.

[14] *The New Order*,Vol.III, No.10, Oct. 1897.

[15] *The New Order*, Vol.IV, No.8, Oct. 1898.

[16] *The New Order*,Vol.IV, No.1, Feb. 1898.

[17] Hubert Hammond, in *The New Order*,Vol.IV, No.2, March 1898, states that the majority of the colonists were vegetarian, in some cases on grounds of principle, in others of frugality, but that others remained meat-eaters.

18 *Essex County Chronicle*, 12 Nov. 1897.

19 Hocking, S.: *op. cit.*, pp.149-151.

20 *Seed-Time*, April 1895.

21 *The New Order*, Vol. III, Nos. 5 and 6, May and June 1897.

22 Hocking, S.: *op. cit.*, p.107.

23 The location of Hocking's colony, named 'Strangeways' in the novel, has sometimes mistakenly been identified with the later Whiteway colony in Gloucestershire, but given the presence on the fringes of her colony of 'Wallace Glacier', clearly a portrait of Aylmer Maude, and 'Michael Kovalevsky', a stand-in for Tchertkoff (both of whom had now moved to Essex), there can be no doubting its identification with Purleigh.

Chapter 4
DISTRACTIONS

1 *The New Order*, Vol.III, No.10, Oct. 1897.

2 Quoted in Armytage, W.H.G.: *Heavens Below*, 1961, p.346.

3 The Greenwich Park incident came to form a core episode in Joseph Conrad's 1907 novel, *The Secret Agent*.

4 On the Leeds Brotherhood Church, see Bevir, M: 'The Rise of Ethical Anarchism in Britain, 1885-1900', *Historical Research* 69 (1996), p.143-165 and A.G. Higgins: *History of the Brotherhood Church*, 1982.

5 Foster had been a successful businessman in the drapery trade but left it in 1897 to pursue his socialist views. He joined the Labour Church and became increasingly involved with the emerging Labour Party, becoming Labour Lord Mayor of Leeds in 1928 (Jones, P.d'A., *op.cit.*, p.409).

6 This was published in August 1897.

7 Maude, A.: 'Recollections of Tolstoy' in *Slavonic and East European Review*, Vol.7, No.20, 1929, p.476.

8   Popoff, A.: *op. cit.*, 2014, p.123, citing Maude, A.: *The Life of Tolstoy*: Vol.2, p.356.

9   *Essex County Chronicle*, 19 August 1898, cited in Hardy, *op. cit.*, p. 188. A copy can be found in the Cuttle Collection of newscuttings, Essex Record Office T/P 181/8/42.

10   Shaw, N., *op. cit.*, 1935, p.35.

11   Tchertkoff's letters to Tolstoy are in the Leo Tolstoy State Museum in Moscow. Most have been published in Russian in the Jubilee edition of *Tolstoy's Letters,* issued in 90 volumes between 1928 and 1958. Popoff, *op. cit.*, 2014, p.132, says Tchertkoff wrote fifteen letters, some running to twenty pages, in the four months after his arrival in England and 'was also sending newspaper cuttings and updates about meetings at Kenworthy's commune'.

Chapter 5
A Canal to the Kingdom of Heaven

1   *The New Order*, Vol.IV, No.1, Feb. 1898.

2   The details of these arrangements were recorded by Hubert Hammond in the April 1898 edition of *The New Order* and were quoted in Hardy, D.: *op. cit.*, 1979, pp.189-190.

3   The Labour Church had been founded in 1891 by a Unitarian Minister, John Trevor, to provide places of worship for Christian Socialists. Their teachings had much in common with the Brotherhood Church and Kenworthy addressed Labour Church congregations on more than one occasion.

4   Interview with Aylmer Maude, *Essex County Chronicle*, 19 Aug. 1898.

5   *The New Order,* Vol.IV, No.6, July 1898.

6   Sgt. Adam John Eves. See the website of the Essex Police Memorial Trust: https://memorial.essex.police.uk/roll-of-honour/adam-john-eves/

⁷ Letter to the *Essex County Chronicle*, from the Rev. R.T. Love, Purleigh Rectory, 5 July 1897. A copy can be found in the Cuttle Collection of newscuttings, Essex Record Office T/P 181/8/42.

⁸ This report was reprinted in the *Dundee Evening Telegraph*, 26 Aug. 1898.

⁹ *The New Order*, Vol.III, No.9, Sept. 1897.

¹⁰ Log book of Dr. Hawkins Church School, Cock Clarks, Purleigh, Essex Record Office E/ML 179/1. The entry is reproduced here by courtesy of E.R.O.

¹¹ Detailed financial reports for the colony do not survive but Hammond, writing in *The New Order* in April 1898 conceded that 'we are near the end of our resources'. How the new acquisition was financed is not clear.

¹² *The New Order*, Vol.IV, No.8, Sept. 1898.

¹³ Quoted in Armytage, W.H.G.: *op.cit.*, 1961, p.348.

¹⁴ *The Daily News*, 5 Aug. 1898.

¹⁵ A copy of this article can be found in the Cuttle Collection of newscuttings, Essex Record Office T/P 181/8/42.

¹⁶ In fact, Mrs Maude, née Louise Shanks, was not Russian, though born and raised in that country.

¹⁷ *Essex County Chronicle*, 19 August 1898.

¹⁸ Redfern, P: *Journey to Understanding*, 1946, p.92. Redfern dates this visit to June 1899 but the picture he draws of the community suggests to me that it was actually 1898.

Chapter 6

THE SETTLEMENT UNSETTLED

¹ This and other following details are taken from Chapters 5 and 6 of Woodcock, G and Avakumovic, I: *The Doukhobors*, 1968.

² *Labour Annual,* 1898, speaks of 23 Russian exiles.

3 Salome Hocking, in *Belinda the Backward* (p.56) has Kovalesky, her fictional counterpart to Tchertkoff, warn Belinda of the risk of Russian spies, sent to watch his activities.

4 For details of this episode see Woodcock, G.: 'Russian Writers and the Doukhobors' in *Slavic and East-European Connections*, a special issue of *Canadian Literature* 120, Spring 1989, pp.110-114.

5 Typescript copies of this correspondence are held in the Doukhobor collection of James Mavor in the Simon Fraser University Library, Sutton, British Columbia.

6 Maude, in 'The Doukhobors: a Russian Exodus' in his *Tolstoy and his Problems: Essays by Aylmer Maude*, 1901, states that Khilkov was also in this party. He may have been an afterthought, since he was clearly not mentioned in Tchertkoff's letter of 27 August. In all, four shiploads of Doukhobors crossed to Canada in 1899. On one of them the party was accompanied by St. John.

7 Little has been discovered about the background of these two men. J. Thacker describes Owen Trafford as 'a tradesman' and refers to the other man, whom she refers to as Jack Bent, a carpenter (*Whiteway Colony: the Social History of a Tolstoyan Community*, pp.7 and 209). Holman, M.J. de K.: 'The Purleigh Colony: Tolstoyan Togetherness in the Late 1890s', p.211, is a major source on this incident.

8 As reprinted in the *Dundee Evening Telegraph*, 26 August 1898.

9 Shaw, N.: *op. cit.*, 1935, p.37.

10 Shaw, N.: *op. cit.*, 1935, p.27.

11 *The New Order*, Vol.IV, No.3, April 1898.

12 *The New Order* contains several references to a colonist from the West Country who had come with just such an intent. Bracher is the most likely candidate.

13 There is some doubt as to her status in the Maude household. Joy Thacker, *op. cit.*, writing in 1993, claims she was governess to Maude's children but Nellie Shaw, in 1935, writing from her own life experience, while agreeing that she had lived with the Maudes, does not mention this role, describing her only as 'a lady of education and some literary ability'. It may be that Thacker was confusing her with Jeannie Straughan, whom Shaw identifies as the Maudes' governess.

14 Shaw, N., *op.cit.*, 1935, p.38.

15 Shaw, N., *op. cit.*, 1935, p.45.

16 In *The New Order*, Vol.IV, No.9, Oct. 1898, he was said to have been with the Leeds group 'a few weeks'.

17 *The New Order*, Vol.IV, No.8, Sept. 1898.

Chapter 7
DECLINE AND FALL

1 Quoted in Armytage, W.H.G., *op. cit.*, 1961, p. 348.

2 Information from *Essex County Chronicle* reports, 12 November 1897 and 19 August 1898. The plans for Kenworthy's house, submitted to the Maldon Rural Sanitary Authority, can be found in the Essex Record Office, D/RMa Pb1/53 and are reproduced here by courtesy of E.R.O. The bungalow was this time built of 'timber or concrete slabs', not from bricks. A second plan, D/RMa Pb1/54, was submitted for a smaller cottage to be built nearby for Florence Holah, another member of the Croydon Brotherhood Church who worked with Tchertkoff on translating Tolstoy. There is no evidence as to whether it was actually built.

3 In *The New Order*, Vol.IV, No.6, July 1898, Foster writes of 'our honoured leader, J.C. Kenworthy' doing carpentry work in the sale shop of the colony's premises. In April of the same

year he was addressing meetings in St. James' Hall, Leeds, once and sometimes twice on Sundays.

[4]   In this he was successful. A clean water supply finally arrived in 1900, fed from a source in Woodham Walter.

[5]   Undated printed election flyer in the Cuttle Collection of newscuttings, Essex Record Office, T/P181/8/42. The context suggests this dates from 1899.

[6]   *Essex County Chronicle* reports, 17 February and 10 March 1899, in the Cuttle Collection of newscuttings, Essex Record Office T/P 181/8/42; The New Order, March 1899.

[7]   The Alliance Pit was formed in 1897 when the previous operating company went into liquidation. The collective survived until the early 1900s.

[8]   Kenworthy always called his wife Emily or 'M', but her name is recorded here as Eleanor to differentiate her from the daughter, Emily.

[9]   It is possible that these absentee occupiers may have been Eiloart and Arthur Drover, each of whose names appears in the Electoral Register for Purleigh in 1900, described as occupying 'part of a dwelling house' at Cock Clarks. There is, however, no firm evidence that they were still in residence at that time and by the following year their names have disappeared. Harkin was still shown in the 1903 Electoral Register as occupier of a cottage at 'The Colony'.

[10]   On Zhook, see 'Reading Revolution: Russian Emigrés and the Reception of Russian Literature in England, c.1890-1905', an unpublished thesis by Carol L. Peaker, Wolfson College, Oxford, 2006.

[11]   Maude, A.: *op.cit.*, 1911, p.598.

[12]   *The New Order*, New Series, Vol. VI, March 1900.

[13]   Quoted in Kenworthy, J.C.: *op. cit.*, 1902, p.243.

Chapter 8
Post Mortems

[1] Shaw, N.: *op. cit.*, 1935.
[2] Shaw, N.: *op. cit.*, 1935, p.225.
[3] Maude, A: *op.cit.*, 1904, p.47.
[4] Maude, A: *op.cit.*, 1911, p.546.
[5] *The New Order*, Vol.IV, No.3, March 1898, quoted in Thacker, *op.cit.*, 1993, p.6.
[6] Redfern, P.: *op.cit.*, 1946, p.92.
[7] Hocking, S.: *op. cit.*, 1905, p.106.
[8] *The New Order*, New Series, No. 24, Feb. 1900.
[9] Kenworthy, J.C.: *op. cit.*, 1902, pp.16–17.
[10] Shaw, N., *op. cit.*, 1935, p.36.
[11] Shaw, N., *op. cit.*, 1935
[12] *The New Order*, Vol.IV, No.6, July 1898
[13] *The New Order*, Vol.II, Nos.10 and 11, Oct. and Nov. 1896. They in turn drew a response from the Church Treasurer, W.P. Swainson, dissociating many of the church members from their approach to marriage.

Chapter 9
Afterlife

[1] *The New Order*, New Series, No. 25, March 1900.
[2] *The New Order*, New Series No. 30, August 1900.
[3] *The New Order*, New Series No. 33, November 1900.
[4] A volume of newscuttings and programmes of the Union survives in Croydon Central Library: AR 181/2.
[5] *London Daily News*, 20 March 1903.
[6] *The Globe*, 3 Sept. 1901.
[7] The Ames came to Purleigh via Southbourne in Hampshire where, according to the 1901 census, taken in

March of that year, Ernest was acting as 'secretary to a private publisher' – who must have been Tchertkoff (see Chapter 10). 'Blackburn Notes' in *The New Order*, New Series, Vol. VI, Aug. 1900, gives the names of others in the Blackburn group: the Gredys, the MacLeods, with their child, the Carters and Fern Thackway. They may also have travelled to Purleigh.

[8] Quoted in *The New Order*, New Series No. 19, August 1899.

[9] Higgins, A.G.: *op. cit.*, 1982. Taylor had, by this stage, married Elsie Ames, sister of Ernest.

[10] *The New Order*, New Series No. 42, Nov. 1901.

[11] Log book of Dr Hawkins' Church School, Cock Clarks, Essex Record Office, E/ML 179/1.

[12] The Purleigh parish register of burials records that on 30 April 1902, William Andrews, aged 25, was buried. A note in the margin records that he 'died of smallpox at the "colony" premises of old Avenals' (ex inf. Steven Potter),

[13] *Essex Weekly News*, 28 March, 1902, cited in Holman, *op. cit.*, p.221.

[14] *Essex County Chronicle* report, 22 August 1902.

[15] Higgins, *op. cit.*, 1982.

[16] *London Daily News*, 13 and 17 March, 1903.

[17] *London Daily News*, 17 March, 1903.

[18] *London Daily News*, 20 March 1903.

[19] The most detailed press report of the case appears in the *Northern Daily Telegraph*, 6 November 1903.

[20] *Essex County Chronicle*, 3 November 1905. On this later phase, see Higgins, *op. cit.* Jenny Ames later married another Beeston Brotherhood member, Sidney Overbury.

Chapter 10
LEGACIES

[1] On the Essex Plotlands, see Hardy, D. and Ward, C.: *Arcadia for All: the Legacy of a Makeshift Landscape*, Nottingham, 2004.

[2] *The New Order*, Vol.I, No.8, August 1895. This gives the size as four acres, whereas the following year, it was being described as three.

[3] *The New Order*, Vol.II, No.7, July 1896.

[4] On the Ashingdon Colony, see Hardy, D.: *op.cit.*, 1979, pp.196-7. By 1898, Frederick Browne was living in Brotherhood Cottage, declaring himself an artist and an anarchist and being brought to court twice, in 1897 and 1898, for sending obscene postcards through the post, for which he served both a prison term and a spell in the County Asylum. Evans appears in neither the 1901 or 1911 census returns for Ashingdon.

[5] *The New Order*, Vol.IV, No.6, July 1898.

[6] *The New Order*, Vol.IV, No.2, March 1898.

[7] On the Mayland community, see Webber, R.: 'The printer who came back to the land' in *Essex Countryside*, Vol.23, No.221, June 1975, and Hardy, D: *op. cit.*, 1979, pp.114-9

[8] *Daily Herald*, 24 Nov. 1955. Protheroe had married his wife, another Whiteway colonist, following the death of his 'free union' partner, Jeannie Straughan.

[9] On Burtt's travels see Higgs, C.: *Cocoa, Slavery and Colonial Africa*, 2012.

[10] Reported, *inter alia*, in the *New Zealand Herald*, 24 April 1909.

[11] Shaw, N.: *op. cit.*, p. 175, quoted in Marsh, J. *op.cit.*, 1982, p.103.

[12] Woodcock, G. and Avakumovic, I.: *op.cit.*, 1968, p.174.

[13] Electoral register for Purleigh, 1910, and 1911 census returns.

[14] Maude's statement appears in his *Life of Tolstoy*, Vol. 2, p.360, though the original agreement with Kenworthy survives and was published in the 1978 edition of Tolstoy's letters edited by R.F. Christian, Vol.2, p.354. It is quoted in full in Popoff, A: *op. cit.*, 2014, p.122. The arguments over Tolstoy's translations are fully expounded by Carol L. Peaker, *op. cit.*, 2006.

[15] Letters concerning this affair are among the Maude papers at Leeds University Library, Special Collections: LRA: MS 553.

[16] A copy of the 1901/2 Report, with retraction, is among the Maude papers in Leeds University Library, Special Collections: MS 553/30/9. Maude, in his *Life of Tolstoy: the Later Years*, pp.553-4, recounts that the two men never spoke again after falling out over Maude's account of the Doukhobor affair.

[17] Horsbrugh-Porter, Anna: *Memories of Revolution: Russian Women Remember*, 1993, p.11. It is not clear whether she was referring to Bancroft House in Great Baddow, their first house in the village, or to Ladywell House, to which they had moved by 1902.

[18] Census returns for Great Baddow, 1901. The Dunns moved with the Maudes to Ladywell Cottage and were still there in 1911.

[19] Early volumes under the Free Age Press imprint bear the address 'Maldon' but Michael Holman argues that there was never a printing or publishing mechanism in Essex, the production side being handled by Fifield from his home in south London (Holman, M.J. de K.: 'Translating Tolstoy for the Free Age Press: Vladimir Chertkov and His English Manager Arthur Fifield' in *Slavonic and East European Review*, Vol. 66 No.2, April 1988, pp.184-197). Salome Hocking, in *Belinda the Backward* (p.19), talks, on the other hand, of her character Kovalevsky (Tchertkoff) as having 'bought a

printing-press' and always being 'busy translating and printing pamphlets to send to Russia'.

[20] Kenworthy's role in both Leeds and Blackburn can be explored in Armytage, W.H.G.: *op. cit.*, 1961, pp.192-6 and 207-210.

[21] Letter from Kenworthy to Wallace, 2 July 1900; reply from Wallace to Kenworthy, 4 July 1900 (Natural History Musum, Wallace Correspondence Project, WCP 3195 and 5129).

[22] Kenworthy, J.C.: *op. cit.*, 1902, p.216. The date of 1901 can only be a probability. The Introduction to the book is dated February 1902 and it seems likely that the body of the text was written in 1901.

[23] Kenworthy, *op.cit.*, p.208.

[24] Kenworthy writes about both these moments in his largely autobiographical novella, *The World's Last Passage*, published in 1896.

[25] Report in *The Cambridge Daily News*, 13 April 1903.

[26] *The St James Gazette*, 23 June 1900.

[27] Kenworthy had published two earlier volumes of poetry, *The Judgment of the City*, 1889, and *Amgiad and the Fair Lady*, 1893.

[28] Reported, *inter alia*, in the *Sheffield Independent*, 3 July 1902.

[29] Alston, C., *Tolstoy and his Disciples*. p.270, fn.151.

[30] Letter from Maude to Perris, 27 June 1903: Leeds University Library, Special Collections: LRA: MS 553/36.

[31] Kenworthy was admitted on 24 November 1909 and was discharged from the care of that institution a year later on 23 November 1910 (Essex County Asylum, Index of Male Inmates: Essex Record Office: A/H 10/2/1/5). I am extremely grateful to Stephanie Philpotts, Kenworthy's great-great granddaughter, for pointing out to me the existence of these documents.

³² Family records describe her illness as having been chorea, though her death certificate records the cause of death as having been heart failure.

³³ Transcribed and listed on the Genuki genealogy website.

³⁴ I am grateful to Stephanie Philpotts for these details.

³⁵ On Kenworthy's later years, see Draper, C: 'From Everton to the Asylum (1861-1948)', 2016: *Northern Voices* website (see Bibliography).

³⁶ On the Georgia colony, see John O. Fish: 'The Christian Commonwealth Colony: a Georgia Experiment, 1896-1900' in *The Georgia Historical Quarterly*, Vol. 57, No.2, 1973, pp.213-226.

³⁷ The Dutch colony at Blaricum lasted from 1900 to 1903 and followed a remarkably similar life-cycle to Purleigh. On this see Bank, J. and van Buuren, M.: *Dutch Culture in a European Perspective: 1900, the Age of Bourgeois Culture*, London, 2004, pp.407-8. On Tolstoyism in Hungary, see Brock, P.: 'Tolstoyism and the Hungarian Peasant' in *The Slavonic and East European Review*, Vol.58, No.3, July 1980.

³⁸ On Tolstoy Farm, see Bhana, Surendra: 'The Tolstoy Farm: Gandhi's Experiment in "Cooperative Commonwealth"' in *South African Historical Journal*, No. 7, Nov. 1975.

³⁹ The German *Ohne Staat* and its Hungarian translation, *Allam nélkül*, were first published in 1897 and lasted until 1899.

⁴⁰ Osgood, Kelsey: 'Life at One of England's Last Tolstoyan Communes', *The New Yorker*, 6 Jan. 2016.

⁴¹ Redfern, P.: *op. cit.*, 1946, p.95.

⁴² Kenworthy, J.C.: *The Anatomy of Misery*, 1895, p. 92.

Appendix I
Constitution of the Purleigh Colony, 1899

1   This document was printed in *The New Order* in October 1899.
2   What appears to be a typescript draft of this document survives in the Essex Record Office (T/P 180/2). Significantly, the word 'unanimous' appears in the draft as 'majority'.

Appendix II
Approximate Statement of the Funds of Purleigh Colony

1   This rough document was drawn up for Aylmer Maude by William Sinclair in 1912. It can be found among the Aylmer Maude papers in Leeds University Library, Special Collections: LRA: MS1380/1832.

INDEX

www.ingramcontent.com/pod-product-compliance
Lightning Source LLC
Chambersburg PA
CBHW051514030726
47592CB00006B/2264